How I Know That the Dead Are Alive

Photo by Morris, Galveston, Texas.
FANNY RUTHVEN PAGET, HOUSTON, TEXAS.

How I Know that the Dead Are Alive

PUBLISHED 1917
BY
PLENTY PUBLISHING COMPANY
33d and Western Avenue
WASHINGTON, D. C.

*Copyright, 1917 by E. Matthews Dawson
Washington, D. C.*

CONTENTS.

Chapter	
I	Lifting the Veil.
II	The Visible and Invisible.
III	"Never Less Alone Than When Alone."
IV	Shadows of Night.
V	Forging Links in the Chain.
VI	With the Coming of the Dawn.
VII	A Day With the Invisibles at Sea.
VIII	A Chill-Laden Promise.
IX	As the Fatal Night Comes and Goes.
X	Weaving Tangled Threads of Mystery.
XI	The "Choir Invisible."
XII	Defining Soul and Body.
XIII	Visions. Love Spiritualized By Death.
XIV	Back Across the Dark Span.
XV	Writing.
XVI	Soul and Body In Process of Separation.
XVII	Gethsemane.
XVIII	Passing Into the Beyond.
XIX	Over the Borderland.
XX	The Red Darkens.
XXI	The "Power House" of Existence.
XXII	Panorama of Life As Lived On Earth.
XXIII	Mundane Readjustment.
XXIV	Mundane and Supermundane Relationship.
XXV	The Link of Infinitude.
XXVI	Atoms of Life Unifying With the Source of Life.
XXVII	A Soul Relinking With Earth.
XXVIII	As the Todays Became Yesterdays.

FOREWORD.

"Fools deride—philosophers investigate."

In writing this book I am yielding to a sense of duty, that impels me to offer to the thinking and reading public, a series of incidents, embracing psychological experiences, that came to me as unsought and unasked as I am giving them to those who care to avail themselves of the reading thereof; and no matter how adversely their lack of sequence may impress the reader, they impressed the writer similarly when they intruded themselves upon her discriminating mentality.

When evidence of this mysterious force first manifested itself, May 21st, 1911, I was an avowed non-believer in religion of any kind, with little knowledge and less toleration of all things supernatural. Naturally, deep impressions resulted and my viewpoint veered around in harmony with demonstrated facts, but I have no "Isms" to inflict on those who read. I am simply recording a chain of incidents just as they came to me in all their mystery-laden weirdness, without intent of interfering with the desire, belief or faith of any one, as I have even less respect for the person who changes his opinions with every opportunity than I have for the pent-up, fossilized mind that admits its limitations by never changing. My hope is that the reader will maintain an open mind throughout the reading and then investigate the subject thoroughly for himself, as knowledge is never really knowledge unless we *know* for *ourselves,* to which this subject lends itself admirably, for where it is concerned one either *knows* or does *not* know.

From the inception of these phenomena to the writing of this book I have respected a constraint not to read books or writings on the subject; therefore, it is needless for me to say that I am not affiliated with, nor am I writing under, the auspices of any person, sect, cult or society.

The conscious continuity of life after death has always been attested by the universal instinct and believed by nearly every one, as it is the foundation of all religions. Unfortunately, it has been so shrouded in mystery and uncertainty that its solution has engaged the prophets, sages and philosophers since before the Father of Wisdom said "There is nothing new under the sun" to this, our very materialistic present; during which time there has been such a persistence of evidence that we are compelled to admit that there is something, somewhere, not dreamt of in our materialistic philosophy.

CHAPTER I

LIFTING THE VEIL.

"There are more things in Heaven and Earth, Horatio, than are dreamt of in your philosophy."

"Are you afraid?" came distinctly above the "rattle of the rail" causing me to look up in quick apprehension from the newspaper I was reading and move my eyes inquiringly about the coach. The equanimity of the other passengers so surprised and puzzled me, that, somewhat embarrassed at having started up and stared around without any apparent reason, I lowered my eyes and settled down in the most profound perplexity, asking myself what it could mean. Unquestionably I had heard it, as I remembered not only the words but the very tone in which they had been uttered, despite all of which there was no evidence of any one having spoken nor did any one appear to have heard. The voice was as distinctly human as any I had ever heard but no person in the coach evidenced the slightest interest in what had been said. I was alone in the seat but the voice seemed loud and distinct enough to have been heard by those in the adjacent ones—why had they not heard? A sense of the mysterious began creeping upon me under which I became quite perturbed and more determined upon a satisfactory solution of what then seemed the most unaccountable thing conceivable.

After revolving the matter in my mind for a few minutes, still deeply perplexed, I again turned in my seat, which was near the front and faced the rear, manifesting as little concern in so doing as was possible under a condition so at variance with equilibrium of mind and manner, and scrutinized the face of every one in the coach all of whom were concerned, apparently, only with their own thoughts or conversations. That the sentence had not emanated from any of the passengers was as conclusive as the conviction that they not heard. I was none the less positive that I *had* heard.

Then I began to analyze it—to put the search light of reason on it—by what process could I have heard to the exclusion of others confined equally within the sound area? I could feel my positiveness neutralizing—my mind beginning to fluctuate between doubt and assurance. One minute I was positive I had heard it—the next admitting the impossibility of it. When confirmation in the negative was needed the serenity of the passengers gave it, as I was sufficiently a student of humanity to know that if that number of persons had heard a sentence of such import with no explanation as to the source of it, all would not possess the self control requisite for such outward calm. But when I looked away out of the window on the calm face of nature there was something that renewed assurance—something that seemed to fasten the reality of it on my soul. It was a problem I could neither shake off nor solve.

Torn by the conflict of it I became restless, ill at ease and so generally uncomfortable that I removed my hat and gloves (which I often do when traveling) and after putting them in the rack, settled down with the determination of dismissing the entire matter, trying to convince myself that I was coping with a delusion—lending myself to the most unreasonable fancies. All of which was useless—it would not down

—it haunted me with disconcerting persistency—in the midst of my denials of its existence I was conscious of wondering if it was not a warning of a train wreck and of remembering that I had read of such things.

Had I been of an imaginative temperament or addicted to belief in the supernatural, occult or kindred subjects, I would doubtless have been spared much of the perplexing conjectures which involved me but I had always prided myself on my "strong mindedness," so much so that even the mysteries of religion did not appeal to nor impress me. At that time I was an avowed Atheist with only patronizing pity for those less free in thought. Science, so called, dominated me, shaping my thoughts and actions in all things. That which I could not weigh, measure, see nor feel did not exist for me. I was skeptical of all things that could not be measured by the yard-stick of science and here I was, confronted with something that brought the realization that the aforesaid yardstick was lamentably inadequate to the demand made upon it. No, no, this was an impossible conclusion—I could not accept it and tried earnestly to formulate some scientific explanation for the phenomenon but this being impossible, I determined to dismiss it—let it go unsolved in so far as I was concerned. How foolish it seemed that I had permitted myself to indulge in such a mental upheaval all because of some unaccountable freak of fancy—a figment of the imagination.

Forcibly dismissing the subject I gathered up the bulky Sunday paper and resumed reading with a forced interest, accompanying which was a minor chord of pride, of being well pleased with myself that my allegiance to so-called science had withstood such an acid test and feeling that never again would I give a moment's consideration to anything so absurd as a voice coming out of space and projecting words as it came. I could have laughed at the incongruity of it.

And then—suddenly a cold touch was upon my hand and looking I started violently—stared at a detached, shadowy hand, hovering over mine and long spectral fingers closing gently over it, taking my hand within their grasp. My first impulse was to draw it hastily away but something seemed to hold it where it was, as the paper slipped from my nerveless fingers, rattling noisily as it fell, partly on the floor and partly in my lap. Awe held every muscle rigid and an unearthly coldness was upon me. I could feel the blood leaving my face and the strength oozing out of my body as I sat petrified, with eyes fixed upon the weird hand as it took mine into its cold clasp, pressed it gently, as in the act of shaking hands, and vanished. My hand, numb and weak beyond my ability to control, fell unrestrained into my lap, where it lay listlessly, palm up, on the crumpled paper, my eyes still fastened upon it, awaiting yet shrinking from further developments. . Nothing eventuated.

Slowly I relaxed, thawed out, as it were, and began to wonder if any of the other passengers had seen the hand but did not dare to look around lest my face betray my emotion, realizing that such a hurricane within must have its storm signals without. With this realization I began suppressing any outward evidence of emotion and gathering up the paper settled myself back in a more or less studied attitude of composure, pretending to read, while I thought it out—trying to square sanity with such a happening.

Suddenly I was conscious of the most startling thing imaginable—I was not alone in the seat! An intangible presence, indefinable yet existent was beside me, so near that I could have reached out my hand and have touched it (be assured that I didn't). A heavy coldness oppressed me, little breaths of air fanned my face, hands and feet, sending cold waves of apprehension into every nerve, as I perceived the presence moving, space by space, nearer to me, almost overcoming me with awe.

It was touching me—soft touches came upon my hand, at first not heavier than the falling of a feather but gradually increasing to perceptible indentations, which I could feel and see, in so far as the indentations were concerned, but could not see the cause that produced them. When the indentations on the hand ceased, I could see shadowy fingers, so transparent as to be scarcely perceptible, more of a suggestion than a reality, moving up my arm, touching lightly as they went. A moment later I felt them distinctly on my face, first on the forehead, then, in a patting, caressing way, on the cheeks. At every point of contact a cold impression remained, despite the fact that the spectral fingers had become humanly warm, which outweighed in "creepiness" the touch of the cold.

Distinctly came the impression as of an open hand passing over my hair, as though smoothing it back in a caressing way (producing anything but a caressing effect). My whole being seemed slipping into unconsciousness, as I struggled against the perturbing mystery, trying to keep ever uppermost in my mind that I was not alone but one of many passengers and must therefore regulate my actions accordingly, maintaining outward calm regardless of what was raging within, which seemed the most trying test ever put upon my self control, especially so when that great, weird, awe-inspiring presence came nearer and nearer, until I could feel its body pressing heavily against mine as it stood beside me. As I waited in agonized suspense two hands, instead of one, were caressing my hair, then two cold palms were taking my face between themselves—after a moment there was a gentle lifting pressure and I knew my head was being thrown back—my face lifted. I looked up and caught the faintest glimpse of dark, luminous, detached eyes looking down into mine—the eyes were all I saw—the outline of the face shading into nothingness.

I could feel the pressure withdraw and lowered my eyes quickly, turning my face away toward the window, fearing it mirrored my agitation of mind, which might subject me to the criticism to any who might be observing. Thus I sat rigidly—almost incapable of movement, held apparently by a power stronger than my ability to move or to think coherently; therefore, for the time being, I did neither, while ardently desiring to do both. Meantime that unearthly being in all of its weird persistence, pressed its touches, its caresses upon me until awe merged into resignation and resignation into indifference—a feeling that I must endure that which I was powerless to control.

With the coming of this resignation the shadowy fingers ceased their manipulations, the weird presence sat down beside me. I knew it was there—could have put my hand upon it without looking around, but instead with my hand resting on the window sill I continued to look straight out over the green fields and the grazing cattle, not daring to think or trying to explain it to myself—even then I realized it was the one thing of all things I preferred not accepting —the demonstrated existence of the so-called supernatural.

This most undesirable mental constraint was interrupted by a voice, softly calling my name—"Fanny." Instinctively I turned toward the presence beside me in a listening attitude without even a suggestion of fear or uncertainty. The mystery of the voice was solved.

For some seconds I waited in listening attitude but as nothing further was said, I relaxed and would have resumed my position, looking out the window, but was arrested by a voice in pleasant challenge:

"You were not afraid, were you?"

"No; but woefully mystified," I answered mentally, that is *thought* it, feeling that if this apparition, creature, being, ghost or goblin, or whatever it was, could not hear without my attracting the attention of the passengers by speaking aloud to that which was to them not only unseen but unrecognizable in any way, conversation would either have to be dispensed with entirely or conducted on a one-sided basis, as it was very evident that I alone heard the voice or was conscious of the presence. However, to thoroughly satisfy myself on this point I looked the passengers over carefully again confirming my conclusion, which, while it increased the mystery, was a mental relief, as I felt that I could better cope with it alone than to attract attention to that which I could not any more explain to myself than I could to any one else.

I wondered somewhat resentfully why I had been left to puzzle and conjecture over the source of the voice, when evidently the author of it was there all the time and could have spared me the mental disturbance to which I had been subjected. My thoughts were answered as though I had spoken.

"It was better so."

My grievance vanished at the sound of the voice, so human, clear and distinct that the strangeness grew upon me that I was the only one who *could* hear it—it seemed so unreasonable. Again my thought was answered:

"When you understand it will no longer seem strange."

"It is strange enough now," I mentally ejaculated, as I settled back resigned to anything that might eventuate, which was evidently an ideal condition for the furtherance of this mode of conversation, as the voice began instantly:

"He is waiting for you." This not only surprised but interested me. I knew the reference was made to my fiance who was waiting at the Grand Central Depot in Houston to meet me upon my arrival in that city where I was enroute to spend the day at his invitation. My thoughts went so absorbingly to the object in question that I ignored the presence until a touch on the arm came as a reminder that I had withdrawn my attention while it was yet required. I resumed the listening attitude and the voice continued as though uninterrupted:

"He is not coming home for some time." While I did not know just when he would return I knew it was not unlikely that he would be detained many days from home, as he was of those who "sat at cards" in the political game, the issue of which, at that time, was of state-wide importance, requiring his presence in the various sections of the state and leaving little time for aught else.

Here I beg pardon for introducing that which is seemingly irrelevant to the subject but as the seen and the unseen are so intimately interwoven it is almost impossible to treat of one without including the other, especially so, when one is retailing one's personal experiences, where everything points to the mundane and supermundane in their relation to each other as "parts of one stupendous whole," by the very nature of which there are other personalities yet to be incorporated for which I apologize in advance.

Nothing would please me more than the elimination of the personal pronoun *I* in this writing, but the sense of duty that impels me to write requires even more—that my soul be bared to those who read and as it is a very sensitive soul I would ask my readers to be, at least, charitable with it, as it shrinks at every page in retailing that which should doubtless remain sacred only to itself, but I cannot tear out of my consciousness the conviction that there are those who see the light dimly and will thank me for daring to give utterance to that which most of us would lock up within the secret recesses of our hearts with fear and trembling lest some one find it out and criticise.

My spectral visitor, evidently knowing the subject most interesting to me, went on speaking of my husband-to-be and his political affairs, as one who knows, disclosing many things of vital importance affecting his interests, to which it is needless to say, I listened most absorbingly, ever marveling at the wonder of it. Thus I listened uninterruptedly until I perceived the train slowing down and looked out the window into the blue-gray eyes of my fiance and bowed in recognition as he did in return. The train having stopped, I arose and as the presence was between me and the aisle, hesitated as instinctively as though it were a human being, but as this sense of obstruction passed almost instantly, I filed out and down the aisle along with the other passengers, hoping that I bore no visible evidence of having undergone one of the most mysterious experiences that could possibly incorporate itself into an otherwise ordinary railroad journey of less than two hours.

CHAPTER II

THE VISIBLE AND INVISIBLE.

After exchanging greetings with my fiance and his secretary I accompanied them to the Brazos Hotel, across from the depot. In a few minutes we had turned one of the parlors into an impromptu business office where he read the telegrams, letters, etc., I had brought with me from his Galveston office.

While he dictated answers to his secretary, a soft voice came apologetically:

"Do I intrude?"

"No," I made answer, as I was in no way engaged except as an audience to a dictating party in which I had no part, and felt that I had just as well listen to this mystery-laden voice as to sit there thinking of nothing else—how could I think of anything else with the mystery of it so fresh in my mind?

The voice went on speaking in the most business-like manner making me wonder at the knowledge it displayed as to the contents of the letters and before the answer was dictated anticipated accurately what it was to be, adding a preview as to the final outcome of the correspondence.

I was glad when it was all over and we adjourned to the dining room for lunch, feeling relief to be removed from its incessant talking and prognostications. But fancy my surprise when I perceived the invisible presence occupying the one vacant chair at the table! In an effort to shut out cognizance of its existence, I launched into a spirited political argument in which all three became so interested that I did forget the presence until while laughing at a witticism I was startled by soft rippling laughter, joining in our mirth, so human that it seemed inconceivable for it to have emanated from a presence not of earth. Something like a shiver ran through me as I looked at the place where I knew the presence was —all I saw was the faintest glimpse of shadowy fingers hovering over the white cloth—a ghost a member of a luncheon party! It was with something of an effort I again took up the thread of the suddenly suspended argument, simulating an interest I was far from feeling, as I could not get away from the travesty of a "dead" person, sitting as though dining with the "living," for such seemed to me the only solution of the mystery.

In the afternoon we went to the theatre. The performance consumed more time than we had anticipated, and on coming out found we had only a few minutes in which to reach the depot in time for the train. As we hurried along the voice came distinctly, "Don't worry—don't worry—you will get there in time." I just did. I had scarcely settled myself in the seat when the train moved out.

Tired? I do not think I was ever quite so tired in my life, mentally and physically. My mind was surfeited with strange food for conjecture—enough to last a lifetime; and yet there beside me, clothed in all its alluring weirdness was that mysterious being from somewhere beyond the mundane—a being from the impenetrable shadows far out beyond the explorations of man—waiting to add to the burden already laid upon my consciousness. I resented it, holding myself aloof from even the admission that it was there—I wanted to rest—to get away from it until understanding could cope with it. The strain of shutting it out was nerve-racking, and finally I gave up, relaxed and listened.

"I am here," came with gentle promptness.

I sighed aloud and mentally cried out:

"What is the meaning of it—what will be the outcome of it—is it madness?"

A pained voice smote my consciousness:

"If you command it I will withdraw myself from your consciousness and never enter it again."

"Oh, no; no;" I cried, adding apologetically, "I am tired—very tired—let me rest and then you can explain everything and I will be no longer mystified."

"Rest be thine—when you call I'll be waiting."

With a sense of relief I lay back on the seat with closed eyes and rest came with a sensation of being lifted out of or above the weariness by a process new to me. By thus relaxing I had fallen into harmonious psychological vibrations that rested by a mental rather than physical process and while still marveling at the pleasant effectiveness of it, I realized I was no longer weary but in perfect harmony with life and all its conditions. There was a new joy—a new light burning somewhere within me, flooding my soul with a radiance that was as beautiful as it was inexplicable. I seemed to have touched something I had never touched before; a new gate had opened and I had entered in.

With this new joyousness singing in my soul, I listened (my latest accomplishment). Such a simple little act when once acquired—this obscuring the physical and opening the consciousness to the spiritual! In the cadence of music came the voice:

"Blessed be the rest that giveth thy soul into communion above the earth."

"Who are you?" I questioned.

"That also you will know."

While this was anything but a satisfactory answer there was something that pressed against further questioning and I waited for the voice to take the initiative in the conversation, which it did by asking:

"Shall I tell you some things that will convince you that I am thoroughly acquainted with your life?"

"I shall be pleased to be convinced," I made assurance.

"So you shall be," came the voice solemnly.

The voice, in a retrospective tone, went back, far back, invading childhood, to the very first records of memory's tablet and came on down, incident by incident, chapter by chapter, to the very present, giving dates, names and figures, speaking frankly of personal matters, giving voice to that which had never been spoken—that which my inner consciousness retained and held sacred.

It is impossible to conceive of the effect such a revelation can have on one. It produced a veritable whirl of conflicting emotions but the candid inoffensiveness of the voice smoothed away every emotion except wonder. And truly it was wonderful.

When the resume had ended there was a pause in which I felt awkward and ill at ease—the voice was hushed and I was so astounded by what I had heard that there seemed nothing to say—it had all been said. Suddenly a thought came and floated into speech:

"Could you hew so close to the line as to the future?"

"Yes; shall I proceed?"

As I was opening my consciousness to say "yes," an icy wave struck me dumb; a cold shivering sensation engulfed me; apprehension held me like a vice

The Dead Are Alive

as I struggled to free myself that I might answer "no." In the midst of which the pressure suddenly lifted and I cried beseechingly (mentally):

"Oh, don't—please don't."

Quite in contrast to my agitated appeal the voice replied in a soft, dreamy way:

"It is better so."

Unaccountably depressed I turned my face to the window, where the cool breeze fanned it, as I looked out at the moon and the first stars of the evening and I remember thinking, with a sense of gratitude that they, at least, were unchanged, for somehow it seemed to me that everything—life itself—had changed within the last few hours. Then I was asking myself: why did I shrink from the knowledge of what the future had to give; why these shivers of foreboding in every nerve? A voice chimed cheerily into the depression, which vanished as the dew before the sun:

" 'Laugh and the world laughs with you'—you know the rest—this applies equally to the spirit world."

"Spirit world," I echoed, half wonderingly. "It must be a spirit," I mused almost forgetful of the presence, until it interrupted:

"Now I want you to listen attentively."

"At your service," I hastened to assure, as I changed the aural gear from the physical into the spiritual.

The voice began, so human in its every accent that still I marveled at it. From the ordinary tone it began alternating high, low; harsh, gentle; soft, loud; and while I wondered at such a proceeding, it quoted softly in a far away, dreamy voice:

"How pure in heart and sound in head,
With what affections bold,
Should be the man whose thoughts would hold
An hour's communion with the dead."

"The dead," I mused and fell under the spell of its awesomeness, from which I was awakened abruptly by the voice screaming into my consciousness:

"Who wrote that?"

"I don't know," I cried, "but for mercy's sake don't deafen me with your vocal gymnastics—it hurts."

"Wonderful—wonderful," purred the voice, "How sensitive your hearing is—and you really could discriminate as to the tones?"

"Every variation," I replied.

"Why did you not say so before?"

"I thought you knew."

"I was sounding your sensitiveness to ascertain to what extent it could be relied on."

"I could hear your voice, in its every intonation, as well as any human voice."

"Marvelous—marvelous."

My companion was evidently delighted, which fact pleased me and we entered into conversation as unreservedly as any two earth beings.

To avoid any misconception as to the modus operandi of such conversation it may be well to explain that my questions and answers were given at all times *mentally* and under no circumstance did I ever speak aloud, while the voice speaking to me had the same sound and tone as a person speaking in ordinary conversation. Hereafter when I say "I said," etc., understand that I simply *think* and it is heard just as though I had spoken, as *thought* is the language of souls. Had it been otherwise I would not be writing this as I would have foregone the privilege of such communion rather than make myself worse than ridiculous by speaking aloud to that which to the material senses has no existence; it would bear the semblance of madness.

This process of hearing is like, yet wondrously unlike, its physical application. In automobile parlance it might be described as "changing gears," which is accomplished by reversing the connecting link which holds automatic connection between the physical and the inner consciousness, and which by a mental process can be thrown out of automatic harmony with the physical as effectively as the physical, under ordinary conditions, shuts out the spiritual. By this reversal the spiritual hearing, which is from within, transmits itself to the physical sense instead of vice versa—to the receiving senses the sound of the voice is the same. When once the right connection is understood and established this mode of hearing is as easy and spontaneous as the physical—it is all a matter of proper connection with the right vibrations.

To illustrate: the paraphernalia of a wireless station would remain forever without receiving a message if not properly connected, but put it in harmony with like vibrations and messages result. We are all, more or less, unconnected paraphernalia. The same principle applies to the telegraph, telephone, electric lights, gas and other things that come under our daily observation. Everything depends on proper connection.

The spiritual hearing, which is a transmission of voice through the soul consciousness to the physical sense requires as much direction in the accomplishment thereof as the physical, contrary to the generally accepted theory that total relaxation or mental blankness is the ideal condition—it is a listening from within instead of without.

Who has not, in supposed fancy, heard some one call his or her name, and, listening, hears nothing? However, at the instant of the hearing spiritual connection existed but the physical act of listening throws the connection back into the physical.

Conscious harmony or understanding should be established and maintained between soul and body, realizing that they are separate and distinct entities —that the body is the servant of the soul and subject at all times to its direction. The body belongs to the soul instead of the soul belonging to the body. The soul lives after the body is dust. It is the Soul, the Inner Self or Spirit within the physical body that communicates with the disembodied spirits and transmits their voices to the physical sense.

As I listened to the voice as it went on and on I realized in all its fullness that I was in actual communication with a being from the other side of life— one who had solved the mystery of what we call *death* and I was conscious of a feeling almost new to me— humility. I wondered why, after I had so persistently denied and openly ridiculed the supernatural in all its phases, that so wonderful a demonstration of its existence would be made to me. My previous attitude in these premises made me almost afraid in the presence of the reality of that which I had always denied and a sense of unworthiness weighed heavily upon me. A voice soft as music wafted into my troubled consciousness:

"Why not rather rejoice that you have been given to *know* that which you refused to believe blindly?"

"It would be better, no doubt," I admitted, and

wrapping myself in silent meditation, sat engrossed until the voice startled me:

"We are crossing the bridge."

"So we are," I acquiesced as I looked out over the bay, beautiful in the moonlight and rather turbulent for a day so calm, and so I sat staring, dreaming until the water gave place to the land and the clanging, stopping train called me from dreaminess into the realm of reality.

A few minutes later I was pressing my way through the usual Sunday excursion crowd, and soon had reached the automobile and was driven quickly home.

CHAPTER III.

"NEVER LESS ALONE THAN WHEN ALONE."

After entering my apartments and locking myself in I had the impression of not being alone, which caused me to remain near the door I had entered, wondering if any one was concealed within. This was not a pleasant contemplation to one who had never quite outgrown that indefinable awe of the darkness which night brings and fastens upon our childhood. At first I did not consider this sensation as embracing a being of the invisible, but after a moment's reflection, that it did was testified to by a voice saying calmly:

"I am here."

While I half expected to hear the voice it startled me and I cannot say I was entirely pleased, to have this mysterious presence alone with me at night with no living thing near. It was well enough during the day in the presence of others but now to be locked in alone with it in the still watches of the night was something quite different—a difference one would have to experience to appreciate.

After deliberating a moment I moved cautiously into the middle of the room, where I stood trembling in a coldness so intense it was like standing in a refrigerator, this, too, in the latter part of May, after rather a warm day. Still combating the impulse to run headlong out of the room, I stood transfixed, looking about in an agony of awed suspense, cringing from I knew not what—some indefinable something that I knew was there somewhere—something against which I had no means of defending myself. I do not know how long I stood there before the realization came upon me that I must do something to break the thrall which held me—that I could not stand there all night experiencing an awe that paralyzed with every pulsebeat. "Their fears are most who know not what they fear."

Almost mechanically I began slowly pulling off my gloves; and, fastening them together, tossed them on a nearby chair. I then removed my hat, stepped nearer to the chair and placed it with something of precision upon the gloves. One of the hat pins fell and rolled to the floor with a noise that in the dense stillness sounded like a bomb explosion and startled me most distressingly.

With a sudden impulse of daring I passed hurriedly out of the room into the dressing room beyond, where I stopped short, dismayed in the semi-darkness by the sensation of many eyes upon me. I sank into a chair, almost overcome by the many-sided mystery that pressed in upon me on every side, and, summoning the fragment of remaining courage, I looked about the room and was astounded at the apparitions, ghosts, spirits—or what you will—there they were in all stages of materialization, with white clouds playing amongst them, in which floated white, transparent hands and glimpses of faces and forms dimly discernible—and eyes—such eyes!

I could hear soft footfalls on the floor, as they moved about, and knocks coming from everywhere; could feel touches and hear whispers—voices calling my name in a pleading way. A cold breeze was stirring about the room and a numbness was upon me as I closed my eyes to shut out the sight. But a sense of drowsiness warned against possible unconsciousness, which spurred me into action. It was with considerable effort that I dragged myself out of the chair and walked, weak and trembling, into the bed room, and stood beside the South window where the gulf breezes exercised a reviving effect.

As I looked out on the calm beauty of the night, I gradually shook off the awesome condition that enthralled me and could have laughed at myself for what seemed foolish fears and fancies and was ashamed of having indulged such demoralizing propensities as I admitted myself guilty of. In an effort to shake it off entirely I repeated to myself a number of times, "I am alone in this room," even trying to exclude in thought the one presence I knew to be there somewhere. To further this self deception I fixed my thoughts upon the events of the day, the pleasures thereof, crediting to fancy the visitor of mystery, and gradually filling my mind with thoughts of my beloved to the exclusion of all things else. When I felt myself master of the situation, I walked with proud unconcern into the dressing room and began preparations for retirement, my thoughts filled with something more tangible than ghosts and such things, which I kept consciously shut out of my mentality.

I had a most distressing time unhooking the close-ranged hooks and eyes on my dress that fastened up the back and as I labored with it I could feel hands touching mine, as though assisting in the operation, yet I stubbornly ignored that which I knew would demoralize if recognized and proceeded as placidly as such an enforced attitude would permit.

No sooner were my shoulders bared than an open hand, humanly warm, pressed upon one shoulder and passed perceptibly across the back to the other.

In a paroxysm of fear I drew my waist hastily up over my shoulders and sat down utterly overcome. Such an unpardonable liberty for even a ghost to take and the fact that he had the daring and the ability to execute it, was sufficient to frighten one less timid than myself.

Again came the oppressive sense of many eyes upon me, making me ashamed of being partly undressed and I began forthwith repairing the cause of my embarassment, with the determination of leaving the house and spending the remainder of the night at a hotel, feeling it impossible to remain all night, alone, with that spectral horde—beings to whom locks and keys were as nothing. I could not restrain the tears as I made preparations for this unexplainable exit from the house in the dead hours of night but proceeded with unwavering resolution, until a hand came upon my arm and I heard a reproachful voice saying:

"Fanny, don't you know we will not harm you?"

"Unfortunately, I do not *know* it," I responded, somewhat bitterly.

"Aren't you ashamed of such cowardice?"

"But why have so many come?" I persisted.

"Attracted by your ability to recognize and communicate with them. They are rejoicing and are here to welcome you. Do not wound them by being afraid."

"I am not afraid now," I replied, feeling something like a return of equilibrium, if not of entire assurance. Encouraged by my attitude of neutrality they renewed their advances, perceptibly increasing in numbers as the room increased in chilliness. Pleading voices came, "Listen to me, please"—some gave names, others were trying to tell of incidents, names, dates, days of the week, of the year and of the month indiscriminately. It was useless to try to discriminate, therefore, I listened in a general way, while all manner of demonstrations were being made, until overcome by the perplexing strain I gave way to tears. After indulging somewhat copiously, I lifted my head and looked about, to find the room entirely empty, and, as inconsistent as it may seem, I felt aggrieved for having wounded beings, no matter what they were, who had come to me with the offering of their companionship. A voice came in upon my contrition soothingly:

"Do not worry, child, most of them have had existence on earth. They understand, but since coming here they have been unable to communicate with earth beings although having the ability to do so."

"If they would only come one at the time," I complained.

"It would be better so but as there are so few with whom they can intelligently communicate, when one is found, it is an event of general rejoicing."

"Evidently," I made answer thoughtfully, feeling sorry for having disappointed them. The voice interrupted further regret by saying firmly:

"Now undress and go to bed."

"Very well," I assented, and with feverish haste began, still struggling with the embarrassment of undressing before an audience, and put on my night clothes with more celerity than ever before in my memory; all the time half resenting the tone of authority the voice assumed. This accomplished, I hurried into the bed room to be confronted by a real dilemma—that of putting out the light and facing the ghosts in the darkness! This does not sound nearly so formidable as it really was. It was a combination entirely too much for unmoved contemplation. As I stood looking at the light in the fullness of its fancied protection, I heard the clock striking and counted every stroke—it was twelve o'clock.

No. There was no need of debating on the subject any further—to be locked in with the ghosts was bad enough in the light but in the darkness it was impossible—a thing not to be thought of. I remembered that I had a little night lamp, which solved the problem, despite the faintness of its illumination, and a few minutes later I was examining it and congratulating myself that it was in first-class working order. As I tested the wick and examined every part carefully, I was wishing for some *living* thing in the room with me—just anything so long as it was alive. I think I would have looked with friendliness upon a spider or a fly if one had presented itself, but in those well screened rooms such things rarely ventured.

I sorely regretted leaving my little, white, toy dog, Coots, to remain over night at the home of the friend who had cared for him during the day. He was always in the room with me at night, and this night, of all nights, I needed his loving, *living* companionship and ardently wished that I had driven by for him en route home—it was only a few blocks out of the way. How alone I felt yet was anything but alone!

After thoroughly satisfying myself as to the reliability of the little lamp, I placed it very carefully where the light would shed its protection on the bed, lighted it and looked upon it with approbation, although it was about as far below par as the other was above. Then I walked over, put out the light and stood in the darkness! This I lost no time in remedying, and stood, puzzled, looking at the little lamp; then went over, took it up and examined it without finding any cause for its delinquency. While I half suspected it was the work of invisible agencies, I was reluctant to accept that which was more disturbing than reassuring and dismissing the suspicion, took the little lamp, placed it where I knew it was secure from the faintest breath of draught and lighted it with the very last match in the room! I viewed it more critically this time but none the less satisfactorily.

I put the light out again and was appalled with the same result! This time I stood in the darkness, so annoyed, that I almost forgot to be afraid, staring at the place where I knew the night lamp was; wondering at the repeated extinction of the light. Then I knew and a great fear grew and grew upon me until it was something dreadful and I closed my eyes to shut out the sight of anything that might confront me in the chilly darkness. I felt a presence coming nearer and instinctly lifted my hand to ward it off. A cold grasp met my hand and pressed it firmly downward, until it rested by my side, with all the strength gone out of it, and a voice stern with reproach was saying:

"Fear is unworthy of you."

"Did you put that light out?" I demanded, ignoring what had been said, as I was in anything but a philosophizing frame of mind.

"I did," came the voice evenly.

"Why?" I demanded.

"Lest you prove yourself unworthy."

There was something painful about this rebuke, bringing a sense of unworthiness, and despite the trembling of my limbs I went swiftly across the room, jumped into bed, pulled the light covers up over my head (as I had so often done as a frightened child), shut my eyes and listened, with heart beating wildly. I knew the presence who had chided me stood beside the bed, but, I could not, it seemed, remove the cover from my face nor open my eyes, while feeling it was required of me. The very concentrated essence of fear was upon me—never had I been so demoralized by any sensation, when a voice commanded:

"Uncover your head."

For an instant I felt that it might just as well have said "Cut off your head," for one seemed about as easy to do as the other. But after a brief hesitation, during which something seemed to touch my fear with neutralization, I obeyed calmly, opening my eyes at the same time and looking in the direction from whence came the voice.

"Are you afraid?" came the voice so laden with reproach that I almost shrank before it.

"I was, but I am not *now*," I made answer truthfully, as fear had passed away so completely, that I could scarcely realize that I had just emerged from the agony of it and was alone in the darkness with a ghost, who conversed with as much unconcern as though the sun was beating down in the noontide of day. This change of mental attitude was so pronounced that my thoughts kept reverting to it, so much so, that finally I asked:

"Why was I so dreadfully frightened?"

"That you may become superior to fear—to experience fear in its extremity is to recognize the fullness of its impotency."

"Am I superior to fear now?" I asked eagerly.

"That remains to be seen."

Then as if to prove one assertion and test the other

the room began filling with misty clouds, white and undulating in movement, in which I caught glimpses of faces and forms, vibrating, ever moving. Blazing eyes shone fleetingly from behind the clouds; vapory hands reached toward me in entreaty and voices came pleadingly, while I watched them eagerly, unafraid. I could feel their touches, feel the bed tremble and shake under their manifestations but was no longer afraid—quite the contrary. The weird, wondrous beauty, the mystery of it, appealed to me and as I lay watching the misty whiteness and shadowy forms within, listening to the voices, with cool, soft breezes playing about me, there came such a sense of joyous uplifting that the whole earth seemed made anew in this conscious harmony with the invisible.

> "It lies around us like a cloud,
>   The world we cannot see,
> Yet the sweet closing of an eye
>   May bring us there to be;
> Its gentle breezes fan our cheeks,
>   Amid our earthly cares;
> Its gentle voices whisper love,
>   And mingle with our prayers."

"One—two," I counted. The clock had struck two, calling me back to the reality of passing time. The voice beside me, after expressing pleasure that I had accepted the coming of the Unseen in the spirit of its meaning, said with finality:

"You may sleep now—goodnight."

What has this entity of mystery to do with my sleeping? I was asking myself, as I watched the white mist disperse, the shadowy forms and fancies vanish, felt the vibrations cease and listened to the soft retreating footfalls on the stairs and galleries, which sounded unbelievably real. Yet, even then, I realized that it was given only to add a touch of reality to the unreal, that the finite mind might better grasp it. Whether we realize it or not, there is nothing so convincing to the mind as sound.

Then as if going out with the rest of it, I drifted into a dreamless sleep that held me until the morning sun was shining.

When I awoke I sat up in bed and looked about guiltily, half expecting to find them still there. Then I sat on the bedside, while memory, that most reliable attribute of mentality, insisted on demonstrating its power of retention, by rehearsing the mystery-laden incidents of the day and night—incidents that had caused the pendulum to alternate between fear and confidence, defiance and acceptance, until they subsided in joyous surrender. Now as I viewed it in the broad light of day, it seemed a wild, mad, dream; so much so that it frightened—alarmed me and I arose hurriedly and began dressing for the street, determined to tear out of my consciousness what the day dream of yesterday and the night-mare of last night had fastened upon it.

As I dressed with this determination prodding me I was startled by the voice that I was trying so hard to forget that I had ever heard:

"Why fight against what you know exists?"

"Please hush—do not begin the day with the mystery of your voice. Whatever you are, be merciful—give me a chance to adjust myself to that which I would fain reject, despite its clamorings for recognition."

"As you will," assented the voice calmly, while emotions and conjectures ran riot within and I was further away from a solution than ever, as I would not accept what deep down in my inner consciousness I knew it was. With this raging conflict in my soul I went out and while the tension was somewhat lessened by a brisk walk, there was ever the consciousness that I was not alone. All during the day when I came in contact with those who knew me, I was conscious of an effort to regulate my actions in accordance with what would be recognized as "natural"—to be outwardly calm and well poised regardless of the storm within.

When the voice came, as it did at intervals, during the day, it was gently repulsed with a tentative promise of later recognition. The presence never left me —I could feel the pressure of its force upon me while I resisted it—while I denied its existence and was fighting against unconditional surrender. At the same time I realized that a priceless jewel was being offered me: I wanted to take it, to hold it, to press it to my heart, yet was afraid to touch it—afraid to have it touch me—a fear that was not physical but was a feeling as inexplicable as the cause of it. To accept would be to form all my conceptions and conclusions of life over again. Being a recognized freethinker, to admit a change of sentiment would be a compromise of pride.

And thus all day long I fought the bitter fight with an undercurrent of defeat uppermost in my consciousness.

CHAPTER IV

SHADOWS OF NIGHT.

When night came again and I was locked within my apartments my little dog was with me playing about while I changed my street clothes for more comfortable house apparel.

When I sat down to read the evening paper he lay on a sofa pillow at my feet, evidently free from any disturbing influence. In a few minutes he jumped hurriedly into my lap, barking furiously at some invisible object. I tried to comfort him but to no avail. Suddenly the barking ceased, the tenseness went out of his body and he trembled violently, dumb with fear. Thoroughly alarmed I arose with him, walked about, talking to him, but in his endeavor to keep the object of his perturbation under observation, he came so near falling out of my arms that I placed him on the bed and sat down beside him. Instantly he jumped wildly off and ran under it, crouching as far back as possible, with trembling in his body and fear in his eyes. I made every effort to coax him out but he only wagged his tail feebly and looked miserable, refusing to move. Wondering what had so frightened him I looked searchingly about the room but there was nothing unusual in its appearance, not even a suggestion of the supernatural other than a coldness out of harmony with the temperature of the day. Again I tried to coax him out but when he persistently refused his attitude of dejection so appealed to me that I crawled under and brought him out against his inclination. After a little while his fears subsided and I put him on the bed, covering him up completely. A slight trembling of the body was the only remaining evidence of his perturbation.

Realizing that sleep was impossible I pulled an easy chair before a south window and sat where the cool, salt-laden gulf breeze could blow away some of the cobwebs the spiders of mystery had been weaving in my brain, and where lost in thought I looked out on the beauty of a summer's night with its soft undulating shadows without seeing it; listened to the calling of the sea without hearing it; was fanned by the cool breeze without feeling it, enmeshed in a tangled web of mystery that defied unraveling.

Then began a solemn marching, first in disorder then single file, of all the stories I had ever read or heard pertaining to ghosts, apparitions, spirits, and all things supernatural, brushing the dust of time from these unfrequented paths of memory. I viewed each eagerly, analytically, as it passed on leaving a sense of insufficiency in its wake, shedding no light on the present, which half irritated me, causing me to swing with the pendulum to the other extreme and try with all the intensity of which I was capable to convince myself the whole thing was a fabric of fancy—that science could never justify such foolishness. A voice startled me:

"Why do you persist in trying to deceive yourself?"

"I am trying *not* to deceive myself—hush, please, let me think it out alone."

"As you will."

I knew the room was now peopled with entities of other worlds, but resolutely turned my face away and sent my mind backward into the blank pages of past experiences, and could have laughed at the comedy of it if it had not been so enormously outweighed by my intensity of purpose. There I was, perplexed beyond endurance, trying desperately to summon evidence from the pages of the past when all around and about me, waiting upon my acceptance or rejection, was evidence enough to convince the whole world. I was however like the rest of the world—did not care to be convinced.

This time I went far back, even violating childhood by digging up the "hant" stories of my old black nurse (black mammy) with which she had induced sleep when my childish perseverity ignored her crooning lullabies. She had an array of cellar, attic, old house "hants," but her favorite and most effective one, in so far as I was concerned, was that of a headless "nigger" who had "hanted" "de quarter" after the war, in which he had lost his head, and, according to her version, was always looking for a head to appropriate, caring little whether it was white or colored. Here is where my childish interest began and ended. No matter how strong my inclination had been to get up and play, after her assurance that if I did not go to sleep my head would be appropriated by the "hant," I would creep further and further down between the white sheets, scarcely daring to breathe. Thus cold and trembling I would pass into dreamland, where sometimes I met the horrible "hant" face to face, while she rejoiced in her ability to put "dat sweet chile" to sleep without scolding her.

I smiled bitterly and thought with a shudder of the "countless millions" who are sacrificed on the altar of mistaken kindness!

Then memory fastened upon a little school mate who was unsophisticated enough to admit in broad day light on the play grounds of the school that she not only saw "spirits" but talked with them—that they told her many things, some of which she retailed to us, baring the whole story of her little psychic soul to a jesting, frivolous bevy of school girls, who heaped ridicule upon her sensitive, innocent head even while she was telling the story. There was a sting in the memory that *I* was not the least among them.

Because of this confidence she was completely ostracized by the girls and even now memory brings back her little tear-stained face and pleading eyes as she looked at the girls who would not play with her. I was sorry for her but not sorry enough to act toward her as I now would have others act toward me.

Later this sensitive little flower was transplanted to another garden fàr from the ridicule that had made her life unbearable, all for daring to tell what I now know was the truth.

I dwelt painfully upon this incident for some time, even after all these years, chiding myself for the part I played in it. Then shaking it off with an effort I passed on over a psychologically barren period from childhood to young womanhood, where an incident, with practically nothing in common with the present, clamored for recognition, and as it belongs to the family of things not measurable by the scientific yardstick, I may as well record it, although the voice I heard was of the living instead of the so-called dead.

I was away from home, at a hotel, and in the early morning between four and five o'clock, I was awakened by a pulling at my pillow and at the same time heard distinctly the voice of my sister saying:

"Fanny, Eddie Lou is dead—come to me."

I sat up in bed, looking quickly around, half expecting to see my sister, for surely it was her voice I had heard. There being nothing tangible I tried to believe I had dreamed it, but I *knew* I had not and arose with the conviction that my sister's baby was dead, without understanding how the intelligence had been conveyed to me. When I turned on the light I was distressed to find the train was due in a few minutes, rendering it impossible for me to dress and reach the depot in time, which I would have done had time permitted.

A few minutes later a message came confirming the child's death and asking me to come, but the train had already gone.

As this incident persisted and refused to be waved aside as a thing out of keeping with the present manifestations, I wondered if, after all, it was not a matter of soul speaking to soul, differing from the present only in the souls being disembodied. It is reasonable to suppose, I contended, that a soul is the same entity within or out of the body. Why not? I was embodied and in communication with the disembodied, manifesting the same principle under different environments.

As I was casting about for some other incident to fasten upon, a voice interrupted:

"The past has nothing to give—accept the present."

"Wait until I finish the review—I must satisfy myself," I contended.

"If you must," came half ironically.

I went back and took up the thread, coming on down the uneventful line to the time when I strayed into the pastures of materialism, which gave to me the joyous (?) freedom of believing nothing, during which time there came stories of the occult and spiritual only to excite my ridicule. So powerful is the influence of non-belief that even as I passed over this period in memory, in my heart I reviled and ridiculed the evidence that surrounded me. All unconsciously I had gone around the circle and had come back to the present and was fighting it, when a voice startled me:

"And so the review brings you back to the present?"

"Yes," I reluctantly admitted, and looking up in the direction from whence came the voice, my eyes met dark, luminous eyes that looked piercingly into mine, and then vanished.

"Who are you?" I demanded.

"Meon," came the direct, unexpected answer.

"Meon—Meon," I repeated musingly. There was something so familiar about the name that I added, more to myself than to the presence, "Where have I heard that name before?"

"You have heard it many times," came the response.

"When and where?"

"At different times and under different circumstances since time began."

"Since time began?" I echoed in interrogatory amazement.

"Yes; and you have existed since time began but that matters little at present."

"What does matter at present?"

"Your co-operation."

"That would be an easy matter if you would only explain the mystery of your coming—where you came from—why you came and all about it. Tell me plainly what is required of me."

"Has life, in any of its phases, ever been explained to you other than by living it?"

"No," I grudgingly admitted.

"This phase, being a part of life, is no exception."

"In what way is it a part of life?—it is not a part of everybody's life."

"Yes; it is the subconscious part—the soul life. The life of the spirit is continuous and everlasting."

"Rather an unrecognized part in the average life, is it not?"

"No. There are indeed few who deny the existence of the soul—the indefinable something over which the physical has no control."

"However, I would appreciate some explanation, as all this is very disturbing and mysterious to me."

"You would not believe. Suppose I told you my coming was in response to your oft-repeated challenge?"

How vividly my words came back to me:

"I demand some material, tangible evidence—until then I shall believe nothing." It was thus in a tone of finality, I always disposed of religious arguments that intruded upon my materialistic views, never dreaming that that which I demanded would be given —in fact, quite the reverse—I was sure it would not. And now being actually confronted with the very thing that I had demanded I was loath to accept it, but there was nothing else to do. I had weighed my little store of knowledge or rather store of little knowledge in the balance and found it wanting.

With this realization full upon me I arose, slowly turned about and faced the forces that were confronting me, leaving the will-o-the-wisps of the past to the oblivion to which the present consigned them. There was no demonstration—they were waiting with the patience born only of assurance—over all was an unearthly stillness and a "cold creepiness" that made me shrink a little as I stood hesitating, waiting for I knew not what. A cold hand took mine with a gentle pressure that seemed to impel me forward, as a voice was saying:

"Come, bathe in the light of the victory that is yours."

As I wondered at a sentence so strange, many voices took up the call "come—come," until the echo floated back from afar to the accompaniment of the softest music and something within me was making response, "I am here—I have come," as I walked as one in a dream and sat upon the bedside in the apathy of resignation, which gradually mingled into a joyousness that comes not of earth.

After retiring I neither invited nor resisted demonstrations from that which I knew to be surrounding me but lay listlessly observing little lights, all sizes, ranging from pin-head size to a few much larger, that were fluctuating and vibrating, all scintillating as they rolled about within the white mist where flashes of miniature lightning were coming and going intermittently. There was something so restfully fascinating about it that sleep threatened to come in and shut it out, when suddenly, standing beside the bed was a tall, dark person, illuminated from head to feet by a scintillating light which came from within and lighted up the body like an electric light does the globe which incloses it. This time the luminous eyes blazed into mine unflinchingly, as in awe I whispered:

"Meon?"

"Yes; Meon," came the confirmation, as I watched it slowly vanish, noting with wonder that the light within which had illuminated the body, was the last thing to disappear. Before it disappeared, it stood in the same spot blazing and scintillating like a live thing as I stared at it until it became one with the misty whiteness, and still I could feel the presence beside me.

And thus, with sleep murdered within me, all night long I drank deeply of this cup of mystery without knowing or caring whether it was the wine of life or its poisoned lees, held by its intoxication until the gray dawn gave way to the pink sunrise.

CHAPTER V.

FORGING LINKS IN THE CHAIN.

When morning came, after what seemed a veritable reincarnation of the Arabian Nights Dream, I arose with a guilty sense of having abused the night by indulging a dark, untellable secret—something that I dared not tell. Despite the wonder and beauty of it I was strangely depressed all during the day, feeling how differently people would regard me if they only knew.

This companionship with the Invisible had established itself into a permanency and I was never without conscious knowledge of its existence. When in conversation with any one voices would come whispering, telling of incidents in the life of the one with whom I conversed. To this was generally added the request to deliver a message but pride always stood sentinel between the message and its delivery. Though at times, I admit I was "almost persuaded" into responsiveness only to be deterred by the knowledge that the object of the invisible solicitude could not understand

> "The touch of a vanished hand
> And the sound of a voice that is still."

During the interval of this solicitude the life of the person in question was to me an open book—something seemed to impress every condition of his or her life upon my mentality—the future as well as the past and present. Another noticeable effect was that while this condition prevailed the aura (or pale light that envelops the body) not only increased but scintillated, moving and changing, sometimes from one color to another. Different colors predominate in different persons and are more pronounced and extended in persons in public life than otherwise. Under ordinary conditions this light is barely perceptible even to the occult vision.

And thus the days went on as I struggled to adjust myself to living in two worlds, eash exacting its obligations, while I tried to differentiate as to where the one began and the other ended. As the other, however, was so evidently a part of or continuation of this, I could only say "World without end," and let it go at that.

One Friday evening soon after retiring Meon came and said solemnly:

"I am going away tonight. Be not deceived during my absence."

While I listened for some explanation he vanished, leaving a sense of apprehensive loneliness which was not easy to shake off. Why had he gone; in what way could his going affect me; how could I be deceived. All this I was asking myself in perplexity when it dawned upon me that I needed rest and relaxation from the mysterious disturbance that had not abated since the advent of the voice the Sunday before, and I rejoiced in anticipation of the much needed rest. In my heart thanking Meon for his consideration, as the physical and mental strain had been intense, I forthwith adjusted myself comfortably and relaxed in the presence of sleep that was upon me without any wooing.

As I lay between sleeping and waking the bed shook violently, so much so that I was nearly thrown off. The dog, with a piteous whine, jumped off and scampered to his refuge underneath, and I sat up, listening and looking about inquiringly. There was nothing to be seen or heard. "Dreaming, perhaps," I murmured—but what about the dog? In sleepy indecision I lay down again but scarcely had I done so when the shaking began, more violent than before, and so continuous that the bed seemed rocking too and fro within a radius of about two feet, while from under the bed the mattress was being pushed up, as by hands directly beneath me, rolling me about from side to side with such energy and persistence that it was all I could do to keep from rolling off. When I became thoroughly annoyed, this form of manifestation abated somewhat, giving place to a weird creaking that kept up so monotonously that it became nerve-racking in the extreme. When it seemed I could not endure it another instant, I demanded of the very silence what it meant. With startling promptness the answer came:

"Oh, nothing. We are just keeping the fans busy—note the effect." With this a cold draft struck shivers into my very soul to the accompaniment of a chorus of laughter which gave the impression of a joke—a joke coming from such a source! It is impossible to conceive of what a weird, "creepy" sensation such laughter produced—the appalling incongruity of the "dead" joking and laughing! It was something beyond my appreciation, yet, why should they not laugh and joke? A soul out of the body is little changed from that within. As there are fun-loving souls on earth is it not reasonable to suppose this propensity remains the same after the transition from matter into a more unrestricted environment? A complete and sudden change would mean loss of identity, the one thing we do not care to lose. No future, however wonderful, would appeal to us if we were not to be ourselves—it is the exalted condition of the *conscious ego* that appeals to us, all of which is a problem that only evolution can work out.

As I shivered in the uncertainty of this new phase of spirit life—a disillusioning phase, I must admit—all kinds of manifestations were going merrily on, knocks ranging from the soft telegraphic clickings on the metal bed to boisterous noises about the room and house. Footsteps were hurrying in every direction; little lights were coming in and going out of existence all about the room. Forms and faces gave me fleeting glimpses of themselves; the door knob turned and shook as though some one tried to force an entrance, after which a hand seized upon my arm so real that it frightened me into the belief that some one had forced an entrance into the room. The screen doors were opening and shutting, as well as the door between the bed room and dressing room, papers rattled, chairs moved about noisily and voices began telling unreasonable stories, as hands pressed upon me, peals of laughter coming ever and anon. I tried desperately not to be afraid but success is not always a matter of effort. It was beyond endurance and when I would have gotten up, I was alarmed to find myself incapable of doing so—something seemed to hold me. This was the proverbial "last straw," and my temper grew several degrees warmer than my body, as I chafed at the insolence. Then came the cry of my little dog, under the stimulus of which I jumped up and weak though I was, sat on the bedside, and called to him. He persisted in refusing to obey my calling, therefore, as soon as I was equal to the exertion, I crawled under and brought him out in a condition of such abject terror that he seemed more dead than alive, which fact added new fuel to my resentment and I began casting about for some means of suppressing the annoyance, when a calm, challenging voice came:

"Why did you not command us to go, after which we could not have remained?"

"Go now and never return," I commanded, with a feeling of relief that such company could be so easily disposed of. After listening to them go and the pall of silence, as the calm after the storm, came upon me, I half regretted my harshness but not enough to recall them, as I did not care to have my little dog frightened to death, to say nothing of myself.

Experience has since taught me that there is a law in the world of shadows that at the mundane command spirits must go at once and without question. This I consider the most expedient prerogative connected with the communication between the two realms, as there are undesirable spirit entities as well as any other contrary to the preconceived ideas as to the infallibility of all pertaining to the spirit world. Discrimination in the choice of unseen associates is even more essential than in the seen, as their mental influence is greater. While the rule of "like attracts like" is generally applicable and can be relied on to a certain extent after one acquires spiritual understanding, there are varied and noteworthy exceptions that one passing into the privilege of such communication very soon discovers, more or less, to his or her, disillusionment.

When I finally returned to bed I waited in fearful uncertainty for a renewal of the "wake," but everything was still almost to oppression, and while I listened for their coming, sleep came instead, shutting out all further disturbances, making it a matter of indifference whether they came or not.

The next day the desire was strong upon me to tell these strange things to some one who could understand—if such a being existed, and in this connection I remembered my manicurist, who had, some time previously, told me of a "medium" she had consulted and was enthusiastic with satisfaction. Although at the time I had laughed most heartily at her credulity and shocked her by telling her exactly how I felt about such matters, now I was determined to find out where her oracle could be found and ask for audience with her. My nails were not especially in need of manicuring but an hour after this resolution my hands were on the manicurist's table, she filing away on my nails, as we discussed this most important personage, I affecting an indifference I was far from feeling.

When I came out of the parlors I dismissed the car, fearing that, as it stood waiting before the Spiritualist Temple, the chauffeur or number might be recognized by some one who knew me and that my inconsistency would become a matter of comment. I was not ready to give publicity to that which had revolutionized my views where they had been most dogmatic.

As I had never consulted a "medium" nor attended a seance nor believed anything I had ever heard about such things, except to their discredit, it is small wonder that this radical departure made me feel like a guilty thing; that I was violating one of the highest standards of my life. Too, my fiance was a well known freethinker and I knew my action would meet with his direct condemnation.

It was a long walk and a hot day and after all the

agony of it I arrived at the Temple to find the object of my inquiry away for the summer!

Disappointment weighed heavily upon me as I turned away and walked slowly home resolved to venture no further in such premises feeling that I had exhausted all my initiative for radical departure from the "trodden path," to which I had returned and was meekly treading, half ashamed of my digression.

What a week it had been! Passing to all appearances just as any other week since time began and yet I wondered, if in all the world there was another who had experienced the marvelous and radical changes that had affected me! Science, where the supernatural is concerned, had laid its sceptre down; the flag of materialism had fallen into the hands of Knowledge; the dark door of death had swung on its creaking hinges, revealing a light beyond which consumes the darkness that makes us tremble on its threshold—truly I seemed to have changed my personality and if it is true "as a man thinketh, so he is," I had. The same to all appearances, and yet how different!

As I expected to spend the morrow, as I had the previous Sunday, with my fiance, I retired rather early, but not before taking the precaution of asking my landlady to call me early, as I could not anticipate what the night might require of me and would take no chances of oversleeping and missing 'the eight-thirty train to La Porte, where I expected to meet my fiance and his party and spend the day cruising about the bay, a recreation we both enjoyed. With this end in view his yacht had, during the afternoon, steamed up to Sylvan Beach, La Porte, as a precaution against delays or disappointments.

It was thus I lay dreaming of the morrow and its anticipated pleasures, without a thought of the invisibles, when Morpheus folded me within the mantle where dreams and realities are one.

CHAPTER VI.

WITH THE COMING OF THE DAWN.

"Awake—get up," came a command to which I gave obedience almost before I was consciously awake and sat sleepily on the bedside, wondering if I had been dreaming. All doubt was dissipated by the voice:

"Get out of bed,"—I stood up and moved uncertainly to the middle of the room, noting a suggestion of the dawn in the semishadows that played about and the gray that pressed upon the window panes. This I noted with surprise as I fancied the night still young, feeling that I had slept only a very short time. The clock striking four relieved further conjecture as to the time.

"Pull down the shades," was the next order, which I obeyed rather mechanically, pulling them full down, rendering the room quite dark. There was no thought of turning on the light as I felt instinctively the darkness had its purpose, otherwise it would not have been enforced by lowered shades.

As I stood hesitating, waiting for further orders, as it were, I was directed to take a footstool to a given point in the room and sit upon it. This I did without question, realizing that it was Meon who was giving the directions and was pleased that he had returned; but refrained from expressing myself thereon, as something a vast deal more important seemed in process of manifestation.

After sitting as directed for a few minutes, drowsiness came over me, the heaviness of which caused me to forget that there was no back to the stool and my

The Dead Are Alive

leaning against the back that wasn't resulted most disastrously. Thoroughly awakened, I scrambled up, with resentment burning in my heart because of the seemingly whimsical preference for a stool, when several comfortable chairs were in the room, for which I would have exchanged the stool, but a voice vibrant with command smote my consciousness:

"Sit where you are," and I settled down with an emphasis in keeping with the tone of command, conscious of an almost overpowering chilliness, as I waited for I knew not what. As I conjectured, I perceived a little light fluctuating before my face, fixing my attention. As I looked at it, it assumed a pointed shape and began moving slowly away, my eyes following. So it continued to move until it stood directly over a white easel on which was a life size portrait of my fiance. Here it stopped, scintillating, growing in size and power of illumination. After holding this vibratory, scintillating position a few seconds, it moved, with a rolling effect, downward until it paused directly in front of the face of the portrait, where it stood quivering, emitting a light sufficient to make the features distinctly discernible, despite the darkness of the room. Thus suspended, it began quivering into nothingness and darkness was over everything.

While there was nothing especially interesting about this, I sat with my attention focused on the spot where it had disappeared, almost breathlessly waiting for the indefinable "something" to happen; but as nothing eventuated, somewhat disappointedly, I looked about the room and was fascinated by alternating shadows of darkness and light, blending so intimately that they seemed a commingling mass of light and darkness, one, yet distinct, moving noiselessly in circular waves toward the easel, which seemed the magnet. The light would quiver over the portrait, giving just a glimpse of it, when the shroud of the pursuing darkness would shut it out, and thus it alternated, becoming more and more distinct and individualized until a pale, bluish illumination fringed the edges of the shadows, making the separateness more pronounced—the lightness more weirdly effulgent—the darkness as an Egyptian midnight. The darkness would fall into the light like a great curtain, obscuring everything, and in turn the whiteness would come with a silvery glow, giving soft outline to everything within its area. As I gazed upon the mystic beauty of it, suddenly there came down, over and about the easel, a great flood of vibrating whiteness, lighting up everything with a radiance, revealing to my astonishment a clean, white, *blank* canvas, where only a few minutes before I had looked upon the likeness of, what was to me, the dearest face in the world! I bounded forward in the face of this daring obliteration, with rescuing intentions, but my rising attempt was firmly suppressed by a power, not as of hands, but a concentrated force, more powerful and impressive, that forced me down with an emphasis that checked even the desire to rise.

Held by this strange power I began wondering if it was possible that I could be dreaming, at the same time, felt convinced that I was not. Be that as it may, I was not satisfied and wanted something tangible that would bear material evidence when the light of day laughs at the dreams of night. I began casting about and summoning these mute, material witnesses that were to stand before the judgment of the morrow, and in so doing felt a sense of "laying up treasures" of victory that nothing else could give. First,

I noted that one of the sheets lay partly on the floor, where it had been dragged as I made my hasty and half conscious obedience to the command to arise; also there was one of my bed-room slippers with heel up and at right angles to the other. That was all I could see in the semi-darkness that was worthy of subpoenaing. Feeling these inadequate, I removed my engagement ring from the third finger of the left hand and placed it on the third finger of my right, a most unusual thing, as the ring was rarely removed from my finger under any pretext. Lastly I reached over, not being permitted to get up, and removed an onyx tablet from the lower section of a table which stood near and placed it on the floor beside me.

Thoroughly satisfied, I viewed my assembled witnesses and again gave my attention to that from which I had withdrawn it, with the assurance that no matter what developments the night might bring forth these witnesses would stand as evidence against it being a dream, no matter how interwoven it might be with unreality.

As the easel had been the objective of the preceding phenomena, I naturally fixed my attention on the spot where I knew it was. Intense darkness was prevailing at the time. This darkness was like a proscenium curtain, studded with miniature lights, and vibrating with variegated colors. It began to rise slowly, revealing beyond a flood of silvery light, holding within itself the easel, which was swaying lightly, from side to side, up and down, within a radius of about two feet. The canvas within the frame was no longer blank—there were two objects plainly discernible.

Tense with anxiety at to what the canvas was about to reveal, I watched eagerly, as the swaying merged into vibrations, and vibrations into visible tremblings. The shadow of darkness came down, obscuring it entirely from my vision, abruptly changing expectation into disappointment, a reaction to whose agony only experience can testify. I could have fallen face downward on the floor and cried out against the cruelty of it, when a hand was laid lightly on my head and an encouraging voice was saying:

"Patience yet a little while."

With this I forced myself back under the strain of expectancy and sat watching and waiting, while touches came on my face, hands and hair, as though the invisible entities would assure me that I was not alone in the darkness.

Suddenly the whole room seemed to pulsate, the very air became charged with life, thronging with unearthly shapes and shadows—alive with the very reality of the unreal. The coldness accordingly increased until breathing seemed difficult, but the easel, like a magnet, held my eyes, and my heart beat wildly with expectation. Slowly the dark curtain was rising again and beyond, in the silvery whiteness, were the forms and faces of two human beings plainly outlined and I was straining every nerve in the quivering intensity of hopeful recognition. Then a great illumination fell into the silvery mist with various colors playing within its soft meshes. As it spread over the entire room, it encompassed me within its glow, and I stared at that which stood before me, fully revealed and recognizable.

In the quivering whiteness the picture frame seemed only a window and standing out beyond it, looking at me with love in their eyes and happiness on their radiant faces, were my parents, who had only a few years before passed behind the veil, which was now lifted that I might know they still lived in the mystic realm beyond it.

No word was spoken, no sign given; and while yet my heart was calling out its love to them they quivered into nothingness. Still I sat fascinated, gazing enraptured at the place where they had stood, yet realizing they had gone, as the calm eyes of the portrait were looking steadily into mine, bearing no evidence of having served as an impromptu reception hall for envoys from another world. And still I sat —held by the spell of it—the hushed, half-awed sacredness held me within itself, powerless to turn away from where the shadowy footprints of unreality had just fallen on the register of reality, breaking down the barrier between the two.

I was startled by the landlady's knock on the door, punctuated by:

"It is time to get up."

The little dog, barking furiously, rushed from his refuge under the bed, glad, no doubt, to have some real, live, human being to take issue with, while I arose and unlocked the door. She entered with a cup of hot coffee, the one thing I needed most, as I was very cold and my nerves not up to their usual standard of steadiness.

As I stood holding the coffee, expressing my appreciation therefor, I examined the mute witnesses which I had assembled for the light of day which had now come. I noted carefully the sheet which was partly on the floor; the one slipper, heel up; the ring on the third finger of my right hand and beside the footstool, the onyx slab. This she noted, looking at me inquiringly, to which I vouchsafed no explanation, as we turned and went into the dressing room, where I drank the coffee and began, with her assistance, to make my toilet for the day, in accordance with the dictation of a *voice* which evidenced interest in my personal appearance for the occasion. The costume selected was an all-over hand embroidered linen, champagne colored, with every thing to match, which made up in elegance what it lacked in appropriateness as a yachting costume.

As I proceeded with my toilet voices from the invisible almost drowned every other sound as they poured in upon me from every direction, causing a preoccupation of manner that even the light talk in which I indulged could not disguise, as was evidenced by her question:

"Aren't you well?"

"Perfectly," I replied hastily, but realizing that indisposition would be the most natural excuse for my distrait manner, I added, forcing a little laugh, "You know getting up early always puts me out of tune, but as I feel so unusually inharmonious this morning, I presume I am not quite well."

"Would you care for another cup of coffee?" she asked kindly, expressing sympathy because of my indisposition.

"Thank you—no," I answered, assuring her of my appreciation of the solicitude she heaped upon me, feeling the unworthiness that is born of deception. Then, as if by mutual consent we lapsed into silence, for which I was very grateful.

How I wished I could creep away to some quiet spot where there were no appearances to keep up, no voices, mundane or supermundane to interfere, as there was a sacred silence they seemed to violate. With hushed reverence my thoughts kept reverting to that which had just given assurance of love that outlives death; of ideals that persist through all forms of life's continuity.

CHAPTER VII.

A DAY WITH THE INVISIBLES AT SEA.

"Patti, I am here," came a sweet girlish voice, so familiar it startled me into forgetfulness that I was wishing for silent meditation, and in awed uncertainty, I whispered interrogatively:

"Lillian?" Not a sound came as I listened with intensity not unmixed with perplexity, as I did not then know the only person who ever so addressed me had passed into the world of Silence. It was a friend of my girlhood, who knowing and appreciating my musical aspirations, had, in a girlish, jesting way, so termed me as I sang the hours away instead of joining her in the amusements she preferred.

Strangest of all came the perfume of violets, which in earth life had always heralded her coming, and as I marveled, her spontaneous, inimitable laughter broke the stillness and I knew it could be none other. The well remembered voice came again:

"Patti, you do not sing any more, my prima donna dreamer."

"Oh, Lillian," I cried, "don't—if you know anything you know why, but it does not matter now."

"Forgive me, dear, I only wanted to convince you that it is really I."

"I am convinced but cannot realize that you have passed out of this life—tell me all about it—what was the cause?"

"Oh, I rode out on fever," she replied in her lightest, most frivolous vein and laughed in that old carefree, joyous way that made my heart bound with delight and the years roll back to the sweet intimacy of our girlhood days, which now seemed so long ago.

"Haven't you learned to be serious yet?" I chided, for as much as I loved her, her frivolity was an imperfection to which at times I did not hesitate to call her attention. "Tell me all about it—how long have you been there?"

"Don't take it so seriously—rather rejoice with me that I am free and happy and have been here long enough to pass beyond all obstructions and go where I will. I often come to you and go to Edgar (a mutual friend), but this is the first time you have ever recognized me—Edgar never has."

"Let me see your face," I insisted.

"Not now, but I will when I come in different vibrations."

"But what is the difference?" I questioned in surprise.

"Much, as you will soon learn."

The honk-honk of the auto horn brought me back to a realization of mundane demands and I hurried out bidding the landlady good-morning and was followed down the steps by her wishes for a pleasant day.

As we drove toward the depot I felt a presence beside me and looking around I saw Lillian as distinctly as I had ever seen her in life, with her laughing eyes looking into mine and the same care-free smile on her lips. She did not speak but vanished almost as quickly as I saw her, leaving a sense of disappointment at the sudden withdrawal of what seemed a touch of reality to what had seemed very unreal.

Since then, however, she has come many times, always joyous and carefree, painting the other world in such alluring colors that I would express a desire to be there with her, but she would chide me saying:

"You could be as happy there, if you only knew the truth."

"Tell me all about it," I would plead, but she would answer always the same:

"I am not permitted," and I would wonder, and would almost resent her lack of frankness, as she hid her beautiful face behind the veil of the soul world and her voice was stilled. She never remained after she had made that answer, nor would she come if I called.

As the train moved on and I sat complacently, I could have transplanted myself into fancy's realm and have been a queen holding court, so numerous were the beings who "waited in state," as it were, for my recognition, which I gave or denied as I elected. The greatest exclusiveness marked my attitude toward them, as I devoted myself to reasoning rather than audience giving. There were too many. The Sunday before there had been one—on this day, one week later, there were many and each as anxious for conversational recognition as the one had been! I had already had a week of almost sleepless nights and trying days and felt that I would appreciate a diminution rather than an increase in the cause of it. I held the doors of my consciousness shut against any sights or sounds of the supernatural. At the same time I was wishing ardently that there was some one with whom I could intelligently share my secret—some one who could understand—some one who could swim in the deep waters on which I floated aimlessly, tossed by the vagaries of its currents, without even a knowledge of its depths.

"La Porte," the brakeman cried, with such energy that it startled me almost out of the seat.

My fiance met the train and we took a carriage from La Porte to Sylvan Beach, which is some distance from the depot. Spirit entities crowded into the carriage, pressing perceptibly against me while cold touches made me shiver, but I persisted in refusing them conversational privileges.

While we breakfasted at an al-fresco cafe on the beach, I could hear the word "goodbye" softly whispered and was curious to know why they were going no further with me, therefore, listened. These words came floating softly into my consciousness:

"All who dwell upon the land may not tread upon the sea." Some were saying, "But I am going with you," while others were murmuring sadly "goodbye—goodbye."

Once begun it was not easy to shut out the avalanche of voices that poured in upon me, but as we walked down the beach toward the waiting yacht I gradually suppressed them.

An hour later we were steaming over the placid waters of the bay, watching the sunlight make gold-tinted pictures on the tiny waves as they lifted their heads in the golden radiance. It was restfully beautiful but the calmness of the sea never appeals to me. I love it in its wild, tempestuous moods, when it is a veritable living thing in its responsiveness to the storm element, when to be cradled on its bosom is to flirt with death, the thrill of which I have known many times, unmixed with fear. On this occasion, however, there seemed a harmonious blending of its calmness with the rythmic coming and going of shadowy beings, who came on and off the boat with meter-like regularity, giving the impression that they were entertaining guests who had come into their domicile. Too, they seemed to be holding high festival of some kind in which they chose to include us. I had little time or inclination to delve into their motives, as I had given a whole week of my time and consideration to solving problems of their manifestations and had only this one day of my comradeship and companionship to give to my husband-to-be, and so resented any interference, regardless of its source.

After cruising about for some time we cast anchor and angled with little success, tiring of which we cast targets and vied with each other in rifle practice. Although I have a medal, won by my rifle marksmanship, the inaccuracy of my shooting on this occasion showed the effect of the nervous strain under which I had been for the past week. I was exceedingly proud of my reputation as a marksman, and having no desire to forfeit it, feigned some trivial indisposition, "headache," perhaps (although it is something I never really have), and withdrew from the contest, and when I stopped the others stopped also. Some of the spirit entities manifested relief, as the noise had seemed rather disturbing to them for some reason.

After luncheon anchor was raised and we steamed on, headed for Houston, which was a matter of several hours' steady traveling. As we steamed on the attentions of the invisible horde did not abate nor were they the only intrusions upon the pleasant realities by which I was surrounded. A dream picture —the vision of a Paris creation—my wedding dress, pearls hand-embroidered on white net, over the softest pearl-white satin, which had come only the day before, kept intruding itself upon my thoughts— a veritable vision of loveliness. I seemed to see myself robed in its elegance, just as I had viewed myself the day before in the mirror with more than satisfaction. As I was hugging to myself the pleasing vision a voice interrupted:

"Waste not your dreams on that dress—you will not be married in it."

How preposterous! I could have laughed at the absurdity of it, despite all of which there was an undercurrent of apprehension, which I attempted to shake off and take up the golden thread of my dream again.

> "But the gold was out of the thread
> And lead had entered instead."

To more effectually shake off the depression that seemed determined to settle down upon me I arose and walked about and finally requested the pilot to permit me to steer, which he readily did, knowing that I so enjoyed steering that I had practiced myself into efficiency. There is something fascinating about holding a splendid yacht in one's hands, as it were, beside the intelligent direction of which her great bulk and strength are as nothing. In about an hour, somewhat tired, I relinquished the wheel and sat down entirely relieved of the depression that had weighed so heavily upon me.

"Tired?" asked my fiance in a matter-of-course way, and sat down beside me.

"Just at bit," I answered, "The current is rather exacting today." Looking critically into the water, he said:

"And so it is," and as if by mutual consent we lapsed into silent admiration of the glories of the setting sun, as the gold played among the luxuriant foliage and wild flowers that grew beside the ship channel that leads from Houston to the sea. The fragrance of the blooming magnolias filled the air with a sweet heaviness; the birds and butterflies were singing and flitting everywhere with a joyousness that was contageous.

As I gazed enraptured, with my heart in perfect accord with nature's harmonious offering, the scene changed—just merged into something quite different. I no longer looked at trees, vines, flowers and flitting birds but was staring with wide open eyes, far out over hills and valleys unto a mountain, leading up the side of which was an irregular path, narrow but deeply cut, as by the treading of many feet and upon the path journeyed a lone pilgrim, trying as one blind, or in the darkness, to keep within the path, despite its wearisome irregularities. This path led into an immense "Silent city of the dead," with its tombs and monuments gleaming white, far out toward the setting sun. There were many graves— one freshly dug and I beheld the lone pilgrim disappear within it and even as I looked in wonderment, the same being was moving out beyond it, on what seemed a continuation of the same path, which became deeper and whiter as it went higher and higher up the steep mountain side. The pilgrim went steadily on and on, climbing higher and higher. When it was all but disappearing in the high, dim, distance it faced about suddenly and dimly but distinctly I saw—MYSELF.

Then I was staring at the sun-kissed foliage with its birds, butterflies and flowers; beside me sat my fiance in silent admiration of the panorama that nature was spreading before us and in blissful ignorance of the insert that had disturbed me more than anything the forces of mystery had yet confronted me with. I could not move my eyes from the scene—a great fear held me rigid—a revolution raged within—I was wondering if I were mad, and there is no agony so poignant as the fear that the throne of reason is tottering in the face of one's recognized inability to save it. I had not only seen but remembered vividly every detail of that which I *knew* had no existence! I could have cried aloud in the very agony of it. What could it mean? What would be the end of it all!

A mad impulse seized me to throw myself overboard and thus end the tyranny of this mysterious force that held me in a bondage that I could neither explain to myself nor to any one else and there seemed no escaping it. Any fate seemed preferable to madness—the very thought was maddening. With this alternative uppermost in my mind I arose and walked to the aft of the boat, weighing the matter in all its phases. When this mad impulse threatened to become a tragic reality, a strong, firm hand fell upon my arm, sending a sensation as of an elecrtic shock through my entire body, rendering me so weak that I fell rather than sat upon a chair, and a stern voice was saying:

"How cowardly—thousands have spent their lives working and praying for one little crumb from such a feast as is being served to you without the asking."

"Why not serve it with less bitterness?" I complained. "If you would only explain things to me. You must know how sorely my soul is being tried."

"The soul that is too weak to meet any demand made on it is unworthy of the cause that makes the demand."

"But you know what I saw does not exist," I persisted.

"In so far as *you* are concerned it does."

"Yes, but suppose I told some one."

"Of which there is no necessity."

"I loathe things without rhyme or reason."

"This is not without reason."

Utterly weary I turned away and sighed so heavily that my fiance looked at me in quick surprise and questioned solicitously:

"Are you not well?"

"Perfectly," I answered, shaking off the lethargy with an effort and forcing a smile. "Such an ideal day we have had."

"As all our days together are," he responded, smiling, as we arose and went forward where we stood indulging in inconsequential talk, watching the falling of the evening shadows, and feeling the witchery of the twilight hour, as the yacht ploughed on amid the soft splashing of the water.

As we neared our destination I went down into the cabin to bathe my face and rescue my hair from its wind-tossed dishevelment. The invisibles were even in there manifesting themselves. I felt myself immune against any surprise—feeling that the surprise element had been exhausted—that I had reached the limit, and had thereby gained a superiority to any surprise that might try to foist itself upon me. I remember thinking rather jocularly that I could look on unmoved if the yacht suddenly turned into Heaven or that other place, equally famous, or rather infamous, as a future residential section.

Then the boat was docking and I hurried up on deck just in time to step off without a moment's waiting.

CHAPTER VIII.

A CHILL-LADEN PROMISE.

We proceeded directly to a cafe and ordered dinner in accordance with the ravenous appetites the sea always gives—when it does not entirely destroy.

As we ate I perceived an invisible presence beside me, but as the physical was clamoring for consideration I ignored it, very much as I had done, or rather tried to do, during the day. But it was insistent, refusing to be ignored, manifesting its protestation by touching me, pulling my sleeve and whispering "listen," until, more to relieve myself of its nagging than anything else, I listened with as little change in my outward demeanor as possible and this is what I heard:

"Tell him you are going to die Tuesday night."

The knife and fork went slowly down and remained so for a moment, then I arranged them in the manner that indicates the termination of a meal and sat back amid emotions struggling with stupefaction. A more choice diminisher of appetite was beyond serving or conception!

"So this is the solution of it all," I mused, as I stared at, without seeing, the unfinished meal before me and heard my fiance asking in surprised solicitude:

"Not finished already?"

"Yes," and forcing a smile, added, "I was not nearly so hungry as I fancied."

After looking at me critically for a moment with a puzzled air he proceeded with his dinner, while I sipped hot coffee to dissipate the cold which permeated my entire being. In a vague sort of a way I was looking at life from a new viewpoint—the viewpoint of leaving it. How new and strange it seemed—this intangible thing we call *life,* upon which I had always looked as *mine*—a thing I possessed, to use or abuse as I elected—and now it was to be removed; taken away with or without my consent by a force over which I had no control. Had it ever belonged to *me*—was it ever really mine, or was it always subject to the power that now required it? What is life, anyway? Suddenly life itself seemed to line up along with the other mysteries—the greatest of them all!

I neither feared death nor was I especially in love with life, the mile-posts of which had not all been labeled "Happiness," but when death, for which I had, at times, been guilty of wishing, stood facing me, ready to take me into its icy clasp and bear me away to some mystic realm which the pen of the historian had never violated—a mystery which to solve was to become a part of, I hesitated—questioned it. Why had it waited until the star of love had arisen in the firmament of my life, illuminating it, making it a thing to be desired rather than tolerated?

"Are you ill?" came the anxious voice of my fiance, which startled me almost painfully, as with something of an effort I replied:

"I believe I am."

He arose, took my arm, saying solicitously: "Come," to which I responded with limbs so weak and trembling that walking was an effort. As it was near train time we went directly to the depot and the gates being open, passed in to the train. I was glad to sit down but grievously distressed, as I had not, as yet, summoned sufficient courage to make the disclosure which I regarded as my duty to make. That he was recognized as one of the leading freethinkers in the state put the mention of the supernatural out of the question, thus throwing on myself the responsibility of any assertion I might make, which I resolved to assume, feeling that sentiment deserved some consideration, for if the transition was to be made on Tuesday night I would not again see him and this would be our last goodbye and there were only a few minutes before the train would go.

Finally in the most painful desperation I stammered out:

"I am going to die Tuesday night."

He turned upon me a most disconcerting look and demanded almost fiercely:

"Nonsense—why do you say anything so unreasonable?"

"I *know* it," I defended in a tone as convincing as I could command, yet realizing its ineffectiveness.

"Well of all strange fancies!" he commented, glaring at me and then settled back in a grim silence that suggested he considered it a fancy unworthy of his serious consideration but sufficient for his annoyance.

My pride resented his attitude, and having done my duty, as I regarded it, in the premises, I put on the brakes of self-control and asked with affected indifference:

"When does your train leave?"

"Nine something," he answered abstractedly, looking straight ahead moodily, regardless of which I chatted on in the most commonplace way of things generally. Then it was time to say goodbye and I said it smilingly, trying to keep back the tears that were struggling for release.

"Goodbye, little girl, I hope you will feel better tomorrow," he said rather wearily and left me. A last goodbye and not even an apology of sentiment—not even an extra pressure of the hand!

As the train moved out I was sorely depressed—the banks of my eyes kept overflowing with a salt mist over which I had no control, as I dreamed tear-stained dreams to the accompaniment of an aching heart. Possibly I was nervous and supersensitive, but my heart cried out for *human* sympathy—*human* understanding. I felt though that I had passed out beyond that forever—that I was a creature of another realm.

Any storm, emotional or otherwise, must spend itself, and generally the more intense it is the sooner it is over—so it was in this instance. I seemed gradually to come back to earth and to wrap myself about with that indefinable foolish thing that we are so pleased to call "pride," bolstered up by which I was becoming aggressively independent in thought, when Meon interrupted:

"He is more unhappy than you are because he cannot understand what caused you to make such a startling statement."

Someway I resented Meon's interference in a matter so exclusively personal and replied with dismissal in my intention:

"It was *human* sympathy I felt the need of—now I want none."

"I understand," came softly, "you who have always been rather indifferent to human sympathy find it tonight the most desired thing on earth."

"So it seems," I admitted rather reluctantly, as, with a sigh I lay back on the seat and closed my eyes with a feeling of being alone in the world, which

I indulged in its highest key, until a voice broke the discord:

"When you reach Galveston go to his office and write according to the dictation which will be given you."

"Very well," I assented, wondering what other dreadful thing would be placed upon the already overburdened records of the day. I was, however, strangely ready to yield myself to any of its requirements, as the force which impelled me was as fascinating as it was potent.

The train being long delayed I did not reach Galveston until after ten o'clock. Upon my arrival I took a cab which was waiting at the curb and drove to the house to get the landlady and her husband to go with me to the office as it was entirely too late to go alone.

A few minutes later we were in the office and I was ready to execute that which was required of me.

After the windows were raised and fans turned on I sat down and began writing according to the dictation of the voice that was to my companions inaudible. I had explained to them that it was a "matter of business that admitted of no delay," and, no matter what they thought they were courteous enough to make no comment. The writing concerned the disposal of my personal property and personal matters not of interest to one not intimately concerned, therefore, it is useless to inflict the reader with such details. To me it was a very serious matter.

As the midnight hour approached a warning voice came:

"Tarry not—you will not be supported after twelve o'clock." I glanced at the clock—it was eleven-thirty. I resumed writing and continued until a slight touch on the hand attracted my attention to a small, white, transparent hand hovering over mine, as in the act of removing the pen from my fingers and a voice was saying:

"Mind lest you be too late."

It was seven minutes to twelve when I arose, saying:

"We will go now."

The windows were lowered, the fans shut off, the doors locked and we started down the steps, with an invisible hand pressing my arm firmly, as though assisting me. Then I heard the clock striking, one, two, three—I counted mechanically, dimly realizing that it was twelve o'clock, the hour against which I had been warned but without realizing the import until I felt myself sinking, sinking—falling into space.

CHAPTER IX.

AS THE FATAL NIGHT COMES AND GOES.

What my consciousness next recorded was like unto a dream, vague and unrealistic—I seemed to hear the dearest voice in the world coming as from afar, and I was weary—too weary to differentiate between dreaming and reality. Finally my eyes slowly opened and dimly I could discern my fiance sitting near, but I could neither speak nor move. Noting my open eyes he came quickly to the bed and asked eagerly:

"How are you, little girl?"

I tried but could not answer—his voice still seemed far away and I had the impression of having to come a very long distance before I could respond and so remained for some time until the "pressure" of distance gave way and I could feel his warm hand holding my icy one, of which before I was not conscious. It seemed I had just come out from under a great burden and a thrill of joy passed over me as I noted the pleasure mirrored in his face at my return to consciousness. I smiled with an effort and almost drifted out again as I was very weak and dominated by a sense of belonging to another world, the requirements of which were paramount. Thus for a long time I remained in semi-consciousness, ready to pass into another realm or remain in this with equal indifference—nothing seemed to matter. After a long time I aroused myself sufficiently to ask:

"I thought you were going North at nine something."

"Your indisposition so worried me that I remained

over and was not surprised when the long distance call came for me."

"I am glad you came," I said closing my eyes again too weary for further thought or conversation, but was conscious of an undercurrent of pleasure that he was there—that after all he did take what I said about dying Tuesday night with the seriousness that I felt it deserved.

All that day and night the invisibles hovered about me. I could feel their touches, hear their voices whispering softly as they came and went, touching my fevered brow with their cold fingers. I slept intermittently, my dreams were peopled with creatures of other worlds and how realistic they seemed!

Then came Tuesday, the day of destiny, the day of fate, but even this mattered little, the tide was going out and I was drifting with it in utter disregard.

In the evening when my beloved was leaving he said:

"Goodnight, and happy dreams—until tomorrow."

"Tomorrow" lingered in a tantalizing way long after he had gone and I mentally reiterated "tomorrow—tomorrow," wondering vaguely what the morrow would really bring, and as if a part of the half dream I heard Mrs. P—the landlady, telling the doctor over the phone that I was resting well and that she would call him first thing tomorrow—again I repeated "tomorrow—tomorrow," as though it were an incantation which would reveal in advance the hidden mysteries of the day with all of its necrological aspects in which I would be the central figure. It was very pleasing and I remember repeating to myself:

It seems most strange that men should fear to
   die;
Seeing that Death, a necessary end
Will come when it will come.

"Please do not sit up with me, it is useless. You sat up all last night and I know you are tired and sleepy, I said to Mrs. P, as she came and sat beside the bed in the semi-darkness.

"I would not think of leaving you alone as sick as you are—I slept a while this afternoon."

"Come then and lie on the bed beside me—I will call you if need be." At first she refused, but yielded when she realized that I was determined, and without removing her clothing lay down beside me, protesting:

"I would much rather sit up—I'm afraid I'll go to sleep lying down."

"I will call you, I promise, if need be," I reassured her, for of all kind women she was the kindest, and would have watched over me all night without a moment's rest, rejoicing in her ability to help some one who needed her—a splendid example of unselfishness.

The deep quiet of the night had settled slowly down and I waited with a calmness that was almost indifference for anything that might eventuate.

Music! just a few notes at first, then soft, mellow strains, so low and far away that I had to consciously shut out all other sounds and lift up my inner self, as it were, to hear, and even then it was tantalizingly indefinable. Little lights suggestive of miniature lightning flashes were coming in and going out of existence giving a suspicion of electricity in the atmosphere. Also, there were little round lights rolling easily about amid the usual white and color-tinted clouds that floated undulatingly, and emitted cold breaths of air, which made me shiver ever and anon. Caressing voices seemed to come from everywhere as beautiful, diophanous forms passed and re-passed, beings which long ago my childish fancy would have painted "angels,"—just a dream page from the long-forgotten book of childhood.

Thus half dreaming, half waking, I passed into the sleep from which I expected to awaken in another world (for which I was neither glad nor sorry), and which was just a drifting out beyond consciousness as an unanchored boat might drift out from the shore.

The next thing I remember I was sitting bolt upright in bed staring about in interrogatory wonderment—what was it that had awakened me in so startling a manner? The impression was that I had heard a most terrific blast as of a shrill whistle. A firm voice reminded me that I had gone to sleep with the expectation of awakening in another realm:

"Fanny, are you ready to come?"

"I am," I replied in perfect confidence as I settled myself back on the pillows which Mrs. P had readjusted, she having been awakened by my sudden springing up. To her inquiry as to what the matter was, I replied:

"Dreaming, I presume," which seemed to satisfy her, as she resumed her place beside me and I gave my attention to the presence whom I felt had come concerning that to which all roads in life lead—death.

"Are you not over-confident?" came an unexpected query.

"I think not—I am perfectly resigned."

"Suppose that to be one of the least of the requirements?"

"I have taken little thought as to what might or might not be required of me. I was told that I would die tonight and feel that I am ready to do so," I replied, somewhat defensively, as I began to wonder if, after all, there were exactions from the other world before beings of this could pass into it with advantage to themselves.

I listened eagerly for a reply but none came; instead a chilly silence, painful in its intensity, seemed to permeate everything. There was something of apprehensive bitterness in my heart as I waited until I became weary of waiting, calling vainly into the dark silence for the messenger whom I felt needlessly delayed his coming.

Then the voice came so suddenly it startled me:

"So you are positive you are ready to come?"

"I *think* so—doubtless you *know*," with rising sarcasm.

"I do," came the decisive answer—then slowly and impressively, *"know that you are not."*

"I was told that I was to die tonight," I reminded, feeling that some defense was necessary.

"Are there no other *Tuesday* nights?"

"Yes," I admitted, realizing with disappointment that I had erred in accepting this night as the one intended. Orthodox religious teachings to the contrary, I had never seriously considered the necessity of making preparations for an entry into the life or condition beyond what we term "death," and I failed to understand why I should be detained in this phase of life when I felt willing and ready to pass beyond it. After considering the matter a few minutes and casually reviewing my past life, from which no crimes sprang up to accuse me, I asked:

"Would you mind indicating some of the offenses which delay me here?"

"Practically all the crimes and offenses in the world can be covered by one little word—selfishness."

"Surely you do not insinuate that I am selfish. I have always considered myself quite generous."

"There is no virtue in generosity to those whom we love or those to whom it is due, but to those who *need* our generosity." And the voice trailed off into a sadness that touched a vulnerable spot somewhere within me and I shrank in a self-condemnatory way, for I remembered that I had been rather remiss in considering those in life less fortunate than myself; the fact that I could trace my ancestry back to when the centuries were few had always appealed to me much more strongly than that which today I know is the greatest possibility and privilege of humanity —the brotherhood of man. I needed no accuser; my own conscience was sufficient and made me intensely uncomfortable, as I thought of the many good deeds I might have done and didn't. Vain regret is not a desirable companion when Azrael stands beside the bed.

> It isn't the things you do, dear,
> Its the things you leave undone
> That gives you the bit of heartache
> At the setting of the sun.

Then came a question more disconcerning than all things else:

"What of your free-thinking?"

"I was—er—but," I began floundering under the

weight of self condemnation, "but, *now* I know different."

"Rather late, is it not?"

"So it is," I admitted, and an awful agonizing moment passed before the voice came again:

"That is not so bad. Thought is as much a matter of evolution as anything else—in fact more so. The truth which is to liberate the world is actually waiting upon thought evolution."

A great joyousness flooded my soul—had I heard aright? That there was no condemnation for me who had dared to say to God, "If there be a God—if there be a hereafter—I demand some tangible evidence." The evidence had certainly been given and yet such a demand required no retribution!! It seemed incredible—but what was the meaning of "truth waiting upon thought evolution to liberate the world?" I had waded out into very deep water and the only refuge I had was the return to my mental attitude of chafing because I had to wait at least another week to solve the mystery of mysteries, feeling that if "free-thinking" was no offense I had committed no others and my soul was crying out "why not tonight?"

"When you understand you will be thankful that there are other Tuesday nights," came the voice solemnly, but I could not bring myself to feel thankful for that which seemed to me so depressingly unnecessary. In the heaviness of disappointment sleep began "weighing my eyelids down," but just as I was crossing the mystic bridge between sleeping and waking, the voice called me back with a question so seemingly frivolous that I fancied I had not heard aright—it was repeated:

"If you gave a box party at the theatre would you go as you are or would you dress for the occasion?"

"Dress for the occasion, of course," I made answer promptly, wondering what spirits had to do with theatres and vice versa.

"Yet you would permit your soul to enter into a far greater throng inappropriately clad?"

"I do not know how a soul should be clothed," I replied after a moment's hesitation, then added irrelevantly, "We have no soul-tailors on earth."

"Each soul is its own tailor—the garments are of the soul's own weaving," came solemnly.

"Are they hard to make?" I asked, half derisively.

"That depends on the soul to be fitted."

"Mine, for instance," I persisted irreverently, suppressing a perverse amusement, which was doubtless as foolish as it was ill-timed.

"Permit me to suggest that this is a very serious matter—certainly not one for your amusement," came the voice in cold, stern rebuke, which sobered me so suddenly that it seemed to blast all humor out of my system for all time.

"Forgive me, please—my disappointment at remaining on earth after I was so sure of leaving it is the only defense I have to offer for my rudeness," I pleaded, a deep penitence spreading over me as I realized that subconsciously I was exercising the resentment I felt for being alive after the hour in which I expected transition had come and gone.

The voice came gently:

"That is well; now we can take up the subject with the seriousness it demands."

"I am listening," I said meekly, settling down to the seriousness I felt was required of me (and it was no pretense). I had had my lesson.

"No error," began the voice, clear and soft, "must enter into the weaving of such garments—one false thread and the weaving must all be done over again and thus cycles of time are wasted—the goal is perfection."

"I will abide by your instructions."

"The simplicity of which will doubtless disappoint you, but remember 'he who is faithful in little will be faithful in much'—the little things of everyday life are really the great things—the soul tests."

"I pledge my faith in all things great and small," I made avowal and my soul was strong in the promise of fulfillment.

"A pledge cannot be violated—it were better had you made no pledge, but having made it you must abide thereby."

"I intend to."

That the requirements, according to our mundane conceptions, were not elaborate, we must admit, as they are practically covered by the following, to-wit:

(1) The Golden Rule (the law of action).

(2) Unselfish, helpful love, embracing all *living* things (the law of sentiment).

(3) A recognition of *oneness* with Infinity, in all the word implies (embracing all mankind) (the law of Divinity).

Then followed what one might call *personal* instructions. A daily bath was a requirement which admitted of no interference; moderation and self control in all things and under all conditions; pureness of thought; truthfulness of tongue, serenity of mind. Patience and endurance were impressed as virtues everlasting. A ready willingness to pass from this life into the next as though it were but a conscious continuation of this in a higher, better sense was the last injunction. It was impressed upon me that the earth-life, lived in accordance with the foregoing, breeds no complications in the Hereafter for there are no chains binding us to our previous actions.

I considered all that had been said to me very seriously and reviewed it carefully in my mind, tabulating it mentally that no omission might creep in. As I did so a few bars of music struck in almost abruptly and as it toned down softly, a voice which seemed far away, floated back in weird impressiveness:

"Oh, weaver of thy freedom, be faithful."

I shivered a bit, and moved restlessly, as the words seemed to come down and cover me with a responsibility that was "closer than hands and feet"—an inescapable thing. As though taking hold of a piece of dynamite I repeated cautiously and carefully—"Oh, weaver of thy freedom, be faithful," and as if it required a renewal of my pledge, in all seriousness my soul again made the promise, "I will be faithful in all things." Then the very air seemed charged with something not of earth and I was infinitely happy, as though I were equal to any responsibility laid upon me, regardless of what it was, recognizing no impossibilities.

Perhaps I should write more fully of that night's unfoldments and revelations of strange, weird, unexplainable things which filled it to overflowing, but I hesitate to tax, too far, the credulity of those who read with the hope and purpose of gleaning a little ray of light on a subject which is, unfortunately, shrouded in an obscurity which can be illuminated only by its own light—each human being must *know* for himself. My knowledge can help no one; it can only induce persons to investigate for themselves.

Suffice it to say it was an experience—a night—I would not care to duplicate nor would I care to obliterate. No matter what it may have given or taken, I came from under the darkness of it with a knowledge that while there are invisible entities of love and beauty touching intimately our mundane existence there are also, touching as intimately, entities of the opposite tendencies.

After the many lessons of the night had been, at least in part, assimilated, and the room grew gray-tinted with the dawn, there passed in review beings which seemed expressions of the different cycles of existence. After various manifestations, there were materialized human beings, which disappeared only to reappear in phantom forms, then came the light-emitting, mist-shrouded creatures of perfection, so beautiful and weird it was like unto a dream, following which circling little lights appeared within what seemed a powerful, electrified light that flooded everything, embraced everything, scintillating with color and brilliancy—of which I seemed a part in veritable, uplifting joyousness.

Slowly it all faded out and then there came a few minutes of breathless suspense, lest beings of opposite tendencies should feel called upon to disport themselves in parade, but to my infinite relief they did not—daylight flooded the room instead—the daylight that mocked me for being alive and seemed to demand an apology that my earthly existence dared intrude itself upon its light.

Yes, the day had come and I looked out upon a

world that was as changed, in so far as I was concerned, as though I had in reality passed into the beyond; I realized then it would never be the same old world to me again—and it never has been.

CHAPTER X.

WEAVING TANGLED THREADS OF MYSTERY.

As the day wore on the bathing proposition came squarely before me, but I was so weak it seemed impossible to get out of bed, to say nothing of indulging in such exercise. However, after I had argued it out with myself and felt justified in refraining, that weird sentence floated back in a tantalizing way— "Oh, weaver of thy freedom, be faithful," and the echo of my promise, "I will be faithful," mocked me with the realization that my "faithfulness" had become a shrinking thing in the presence of the first demand made upon it. Then I determined to bathe regardless of consequences.

It was well into the afternoon before this unexpected determination floated into speech, which brought forth the storm of protest I expected. While I realized how unreasonable my act must appear to those who could not understand, I was none the less determined upon its execution—if my strength permitted, which I really doubted. After arguing for some time, putting forth every reason, except the real one, why I should bathe, the point was yielded to me, with much misgiving in which I confess I secretly shared.

After a few minutes I arose, at first in bed, then on the bed side, where I remained for some time weak and trembling, the object of Mrs. P's kind but most disapproving contemplation.

Then, with a supreme effort I rose to my feet expecting my weight to bear me down to the floor, but instead there seemed no weight. A force, suggestive of strong hands, held me so lightly that the act of walking was like treading on air and the putting of one foot before the other merely mechanical. This strength which came to me as a thing apart, yet mine to use, remained with me throughout the bath and until I returned to bed, where the weakness and weariness came upon me as before. Yet an undercurrent of exhilaration remained until long after.

That was rather an unusual bath in more ways than one. When the water was turned on it came with a "sizzling" sound, which I could hear through the open door between my bedroom and bathroom before going in. I paid very little attention to it but fancy my surprise when I stepped into it, expecting it to be cold and found it almost uncomfortably hot!

I came near jumping out so unexpected was the shock. I never use warm or hot baths (except the Turkish), therefore there was no connection nor provision made for heating the water, rendering it impossible for the water to have been heated without my knowledge, nor was this the only time the water was heated by the same process. No explanation was made as to the modus operandi of the heating. Of course, we all know a sub-normal temperature produces the illusion of heat but what about the "sizzling" sound? Of course, some of our orthodox friends may suggest my proximity to a locality where such conditions prevail as a natural sequence, but, as I am leaving much of what I am writing to the construction of any one who cares to assume the responsibility, I will not attempt an explanation where none has been given to me, feeling that every human being has as much right to his or her opinions as I have to mine. I am simply relating these incidents, as they came to me, painfully personal though they are, because that which gave them to me insists that they were not given for me alone, so I am just passing them along so others may know that these manifestations are possible for all who care to investigate for themselves, and abide by the requirements.

How changed the whole world seemed! Instead of joyous anticipation at the coming of my Beloved in the evening I dreaded his coming with a guilty sense of deception, feeling that I would rather have died any death than to have lived to face him, a living exemplification of prevarication, illusion, madness or what not. Yet when he came my unrest vanished before the frank joyousness of his smile, which said, plainer than words, how pleased he was that the night had passed without taking me with it. I so wanted to explain to him—tell him just how it was, but he was a free-thinker and not believing, would not understand; so, perforce, I refrained, leaving him to place his own construction on it—he made no reference to it nor did I.

As the days went on I took my baths without interference as their strength-giving and refreshing effect was patent to all, for which I was very grateful, as the baths gave many delightful diversions. Invisible hands would sometimes playfully dash the water over me, even into my face and over my hair, laughing the while in a light, mirthful way, while glimpses of faces came and went, ever changing; and cold breezes would persist until I would come out of the water shivering, as light-hearted and carefree as a child at play. The impression was always that of children or fairies at play, in which I believed as a child, and I remember wondering if some such experience as this had not given rise to these wonderful stories which are so appealing and fascinating to the childish imagination—who knows?

Then dawned another Tuesday. A cloudy, rainy day; but to me it was very beautiful, as I awaited the coming of the night as the fulfillment of the promise for which I had worked and waited with a purpose and patience that was new to my nature.

As the night came down the very atmosphere seemed glorified, seemed to caress me, and my whole being breathed responsiveness, as I waited in *absolute certainty* for that which long delayed its coming— for that which came not. How endless the night seemed as I lay awake quivering with expectancy, counting every hour as the clock struck, feeling that when it struck again I would not be there to count. Still I waited—waited for the call for which I felt myself ready in every way—just waited until the dawn came and then the sunrise. It is much to realize just how blank and empty life can really be. It seemed utterly impossible to take up the burden again —to act in accordance with the persistent requirements which my promise of "faithfulness" involved. The temptation to denounce it all was strong upon me—it seemed some hallucination or delusion was chaining me to itself—that I had to free myself of it and I would! Rash were the resolves I made and meant to abide by! Chief among these was, that I would get up out of bed, that I would never listen to another voice and never do another thing that was included in my promise of "faithfulness."

This inharmonious mood lasted until well into the afternoon—until time for the bath, which I had promised myself, in all seriousness, that I would *not* take. Then the feeling of uneasiness—the sensation of something important being left undone, began tantalizing me. As I was trying to be firm in my resistance, I could feel hands pushed under between me and the mattress, impelling me upward, as though suggesting that I get up. This made me more determined that ever in my resistance—I simply had had enough of having my seriousness trifled with! Suddenly something lifted me up, as though I were a feather, and stood me with emphasis on the floor. In obedience to it I marched into the bathroom and stepped into the tub. I had passed again under the dominance of that mysterious force from which there seemed to be no escape—and the strangest part was that while really under it there was no desire to have it otherwise. As I had said I would not bathe there was no water turned on, so I took the hose which I attached and used in preference to the regular spray, as it shared less of the bath with the floor, and proceeded. As I sat with the water pouring over me, my attention was attracted to something moving at the point where the hose ejected the water. I looked at it closely but could see nothing but a miniature reflection of my face—what any one would see—and proceeded with the "showering," but the attraction increased with such absorbing insistence that I again took the hose firmly in my hand and held it near my eyes with the same result, only to have the same irresistible attraction hold me when I began bathing again. This time I held it up with the resolve that I would either allay its disturbing attractiveness or leave the bath, feeling that possibly this mode of bathing was not entirely in favor with that under whose direction it was being taken and this was being done to cause me to change it; and not having altogether recovered from my attack of disobedience, I did not care especially whether it pleased or not.

Yes, there was the miniature reflection of my face in the water—but there was something else. Reflected above the head was something white, which upon close scrutiny appeared as a scroll in the process of folding and unfolding. Suspended from it, hanging directly (reflected) in front of my face, parallel with my mouth was a perfectly round, black ball about two inches in diameter, jumping as though suspended by a rubber cord. As I viewed it in astonishment, a voice said:

"When it touches your mouth you will die."

This extraordinary statement shocked me for a moment, but inspired by its potentiality I sat before it, expecting that any moment might bring the collision, which I had neither the power nor the wish to avoid. The ball swayed back and forth all but touching me, bounding lightly away only to repeat the performance, while I watched it eagerly for some time, until I again felt that my seriousness was being trifled with and left the bath with something akin to resentment in my heart—I was terribly unhappy.

The reflection of that white, ever folding and unfolding scroll, with the little bounding black ball, was the most persistent of all the phenomena that came to me, and really uninteresting after the first few times. It was often reflected in water or wine as I turned the glass up to drink, nearly always at the end of the hose as I bathed; when looking in a mirror it was as distinctly discernible as my face. However, I never saw it except as a reflection in which my face shared. Rarely a day passed that I did not see it in some form, yet the scroll never quite unwound nor did the little ball, as near as it came, ever touch my mouth. What purpose it served I do not know, unless it was to keep the consciousness of approaching death ever in my mind, which, at that time, seemed the necessary condition, rendering me receptive to what subsequently followed.

As the days went on I grew no better—no worse—just remained at the dead level of monotony—fever fluctuating around a half degree when the temperature was not subnormal. I realized that I was not sick in the generally accepted term but at times I was so weak I could hardly raise my hands. My limbs, hands, arms, and sometimes my entire body would have a feeling of numbness such as when one's foot "goes to sleep" as the children say. Nothing strengthened me, although I took the medicines prescribed by the doctors, rigidly—I wont say uncomplainingly. I tried to do everything that was required of me by the material as well as spiritual forces, which clashed, at times, very disagreeably.

There seemed a force greater than the most potent medicines holding me in just the condition that best served the purpose of these manifestations. I seemed an intermundane creature, suspended, as it were, between life and so-called death—a receiving station—a creature of both worlds, yet of neither, and reader, please don't envy me.

Voices would come prognosticating things that did not eventuate, telling strange, weird and wonderful stories, all of which I, at first, believed. Then a new strength grew up within me—discrimination—making my perception so strong that I could not only discriminate between the *voices* of truth and deception but could *feel* the approach of an undesirable presence, which I met with the command "depart," and in no sense was this command violated. However, in a few instances the presence would stop and plead to be permitted to come nearer, as though it could be greatly helped thereby—but that "still small voice" within permitted no such intimacies.

When I had become what one might term superior to these deceptions there were great demonstrations of joy in the spirit world as though I had made a great advance—as though I had won a hard fought battle. I shared in these rejoicings; feeling that perhaps this was my passport to that "far country" into which my entry had been so grievously delayed; and half expecting to enter then and there, while the soft music fell upon me like a benediction.

Then the voices, the rejoicings, the music ceased and I waited—just waited on the ragged edge of quivering expectancy in the stillness of the night.

CHAPTER XI.

THE CHOIR INVISIBLE.

The best music is not complete—it ever suggests something beyond—it is only a symbol of a spiritual condition which we seek to attain.

BEETHOVEN.

I was so depressed, weak and listless the next day that despite my protestations a trained nurse was installed. From the beginning it was one of the doctor's recommendations that I refused to comply with, feeling in advance resentment for the constant presence of a human being who might interfere with my companionable relations with the beings of the shadow realms, which I preferred to the mundane, feeling that I belonged more to the other side of life than to this. But really her presence made little or no difference, as she could not see what I saw nor hear what I heard—she was not a "receiving station," therefore could not be brought into conscious contact with the finer forces. Nevertheless I resented her and was not altogether careful about concealing it. Her respect for duty was most abnormally developed as she administered according to the doctor's directions with an insistence that precluded the omission of a single pill. I stoically took her doses just as I did the attentions which she felt it was her duty to bestow, and I always added a few drops of that insidious soul poison—self-pity.

My little dog shared my resentment at her coming to such an extent that he had to be sent away and given into the care of a friend, where he had every care and comfort and was brought for a daily visit to me, at which times he was either joyous in his demonstrations or would not come near me, evidencing a fear that made him very cautious in even wagging his tail at a safe distance. Sometimes, forgetful of caution he would run and jump on the bed, but when he noted the object of his disapproval he would hurriedly leap off and either go under the bed or to the farthest corner of the room, leaving no question as to his ability to see and understand that which to mortal senses was not discernible. He seemed to be the only thing in the world that understood, yet he denied me the sympathy of his understanding.

I was not long in realizing that I was violating one of the strictest injunctions of my promise of "faithfulness" in mental attitude where the nurse was concerned, and made amends accordingly, which gave me the sensation of another victory won, in which the invisible forces made their approval felt.

It was a calm, still moonlit night—the kind that seems to call one to come out under the stars and just weave dreams in harmony with its tenderness and beauty. I had fallen under the spell of it and was just listlessly dreaming—half thinking. It seemed I had attained a fuller sense of harmony with the higher forces—that in some way I was lifted up to a higher consciousness than I had before realized—to a different vibration. Soft, quivering, indefinable life seemed to interpenetrate the atmosphere with the suggestion as of soundless music and a subnormal stillness was upon everything, as I lay in happy restfulness within it. Then suddenly there burst on the stillness music the like of which I had never heard—the whole invisible world seemed a gigantic orchestra, yet there was something so soft about the music that breathing sounded above it as a profane thing in that ethereal atmosphere. It was spontaneous; music without the sound of the instrument, voices without the effort of production, just concentrated harmony sinking into the soul, touching a chord so responsive that it seemed a soul communion rather than a thing apart—the *real* music of which the mundane is only a shadow.

I had never before heard anything so wonderful as on this occasion although it was really not my first audience to the "Choir Invisible." I remember some years ago I was very ill with measles complicated by pneumonia—a necrological combination, at best, especially so, as I was no longer a child. All hope of recovery had been abandoned by my father and the physician who sat through the "night watches," hoping against hope.

It was a cold January night and a blizzard, accompanied by sleet and snow, was wildly sweeping the country and howling uproariously. I was supposed to be unconscious, but I heard the wind as it whistled, shrieked and drove against the shutters, yet above all, soft, zephyr-like music was as perceptible and distinct as though nothing broke the stillness. Even now I remember the very tunes and have often tried to "cage" them on the piano, but when I seek most ardently they elude me most effectively.

All night long the duet of music and storm played on—one raging in its fury—the other soft as the silence, yet each distinctly audible.

When the night was all but giving way to day the doctor felt my pulse, professionally at first, then eagerly, motioning to my father to come nearer, which he did, waiting for the verdict. One long minute they stood both eagerly watching my face.

"She will live," said the doctor solemnly, turning to my father, who replied ardently:

"Thank God," as my eyes opened in perfect consciousness and I murmured "Such music—such music," which caused my father to look disappointed, as he considered me delirious, but the doctor reassured him:

"That is not unusual in her condition."

No one seemed to understand when I made reference to the music I had heard so I gradually refrained from speaking of it, storing it away in the casket of sweet, sacred memories where it has since remained. Yet compared to the music I had just heard it seemed so insignificant, it was hardly worth remembering—it was like the sun shutting out the brilliance of the stars. I fully realize that to one who does not understand, this music is a mystical unreality, but to the person hearing it it is more than real.

On waking in the morning I was possessed with an almost uncontrollable desire to share my knowledge of the existence of such music. I wanted to tell some one about it; it was too wonderful a thing to be selfish about. The constraint which *advisability* placed upon me made me so unhappy that, in my heart, I cried out against the force that held my soul in one world and left my body in the other, a creature of the earth life, a part of it and apart from it. While I did not fail to realize that "in this great moral conflict we must go forth alone," I also realized that it was a grand sentiment but a dreary practice. I deplored being hedged in, as it were, by the materialism of the spiritually blind that surrounded me—feeling that there *must* be some one, somewhere, who could understand, but such an one seemed not amongst my acquaintances.

I wished my fiance was less dogmatic on the subject—but to mention it in his presence was like touching a match to a powder magazine. While I deplored this I tried to be reasonable and did not resent it, as I knew if conditions were reversed and, in the days of my materialism, he had come to me with such stories I fear my toleration would not have been so elastic as his had proven itself. At times, however, I brooded over the conviction that, had he chosen he could have enlightened me on the subject, or at least its theories, as I recalled having heard him relate, in derision, incidents of what he termed "spiritualistic phenomena." Knowing nothing of the subject, it never especially appealed to me and rather subconsciously I assumed his attitude toward it. All religions were alike to us—"the metaphysics of the masses," as Schopenhauer puts it. But now how different! I *knew* I had heard music not of the earth but who would believe it! Then I wrestled with self-pity, feeling that I was alone; that alone I drifted on the relentless seas of other realms to sink or swim as my own strength might determine. This was really not very far from the truth, but it is not nearly so tragic as it then seemed.

While in this unenviable frame of mind, a friend, Mrs. S, came in, and I was more than glad to see her as she is of that rare companionable temperament whose very presence exudes sympathetic understanding. With a cheery "How are you, dear?" she came directly to the bed and sat down beside me. Demonstrating my pleasure at her coming, I laid my hand caressingly on her arm. In an instant a strong force, as of an invisible hand, pressed mine down on her arm with such emphasis that it was perceived by her. We looked at each other with understanding and then spoke freely of that which had long been calling for human understanding. She did not seem to regard my experiences as especially wonderful or unreasonable, and, above all, she did not glare at me as though she considered me quite mad, for which I covered her with the mantle of my gratitude and pulled her face down to mine and kissed it, as the invisible forces began clattering away on the metal bedstead as though it were a telegraph battery. Looking at me, smilingly she said: "I hear them," as she arose to give place to newly arrived visitors, who could not see, feel, hear or understand, and looked at her strangely when she shivered and said, "It is like cold storage in here—I'm freezing." While perspiring and fanning themselves they started an argument about the heat of the day, suggesting that she must be ill to feel cold in such torrid weather. I paid the newly arrived guests little attention; I was reveling in the satisfaction of having heard at least one human being admit the existence of "spirits," as she termed them. It is impossible to conceive what this little grain of sympathy and understanding meant to one so utterly deprived of both.

In the evening when my fiance came he was delighted that my condition was so improved and foresaw that I would be well in a few days if such improvement continued. I refrained from mentioning the cause but assured him that I was feeling splendidly, and we chatted unreservedly of things that suggested themselves without intruding upon the subject that had come like the serpent in Eden, and imparted to me wisdom of which he knew nothing, and which formed a kind of intangible barrier that both recognized silently and tried to ignore.

In the presence of his love and solicitude I would forget that I had affianced myself to death—that I belonged to another world. When he was with me the touch of his hand, the radiating aura of his love, his magnetism, made me want to live and love and sing with him always beside me—"we, two, together," but when he went away, lacking the magnetism of his presence I would again fall under the domination of the force that held me in willing readiness to pass beyond this realm. Listening to the "choir invisible," my soul would lift above the mundane and I would close my eyes in anguish at the delay, as a bride might whose bridegroom delayed his coming.

CHAPTER XII.

DEFINING SOUL AND BODY.

"And there are diversities of operations but it is the same God that worketh all in all.

"But the manifestation of the spirit is given to every man to profit withal.

"For to one is given by the spirit the word of wisdom, to another, the word of knowledge by the same spirit.

"To another the working of miracles; to another prophecy; to another discerning of spirits; to another, divers kinds of tongues; to another, the interpretation of tongues;

"But all this worketh that one and the selfsame spirit, dividing to every man severally as he will."

FIRST CORINTHIANS—12; 6 to 11.

I could not sleep, so heavily did depression weigh upon me. I was tired of waiting and there was revolt in my soul against what seemed trivial requirements and needless delay. A reproving voice intruded itself into my rebellious consciousness:

"Why do you permit such thoughts to dominate you?"

"I am tired of life and everything in it," I replied, as petulantly as I felt.

"Everytime you fall into such vibrations you move the time of your release further away."

"Well, I'll just live then," I snapped. "I am ready and willing to die, but I shall not remain here forever waiting to do so. I shall get up tomorrow and try to forget that I was ever identified with such a torturing mystery."

"Hush, child, you know not of what you speak."

"Then why don't you explain it to me instead of leaving me harassed by uncertainty and torn by its attending tortures?"

"To know life you must live—to know death you must die."

"But there is no death," I insisted.

"It is the name by which the birth into the higher life—the real life—is recognized."

"Tell me about it, wont you?" I pleaded with new interest.

"To know death you must die," repeated the voice so impressively that a shiver ran over me, for the very presence of death seemed in the room, as with awe I listened for the voice to further enlighten me concerning "Death, the hidden, dark way between the threshold and the light." Instead I heard the night birds singing and crickets chirping in a dismal sort of way, and realizing that the interview was over I repeated dreamily to myself, trying to realize its import: "To know death you must die."

The next morning I was awakened by a magnificent rendition from Il Trovatore in Italian. So natural did it seem that I looked about the room half expecting to see the singer, but the song ended almost before I could appreciate the beauty of it. I listened a long time, hoping for its return but it had not come when my attention was diverted by the arrival from Dallas of an immense express package which proved to be roses and ferns sufficient to decorate a banquet hall.

With gratitude to the sender for thus indulging my love for flowers, I had the box put on the bed so I could help take them out and arrange them as fancy might dictate. With this end in view I had all my vases, some rare and beautiful, brought and placed in waiting for the floral burden. Pedestals, impromptu and otherwise, were arranged about the room. Statues were removed to give place to flower-laden vases—even the jardiniers were filled to overflowing.

All day long I reveled in this gift from nature's storehouse of loveliness and when the night came "the scent of the sleeping roses" mingled their fragrance with my dreams.

Suddenly I was awakened—wide awake without any apparent cause. After listening for a few minutes into the "silence" without hearing anything I looked about but could see nothing and decided that I had only awakened just as any one might. After breathing deeply of the scent of the roses I would have slept again but a voice which seemed nearer than usual said firmly:

"Arise and move that table to your bedside."

I heard but doubted the evidence of my hearing, as the onyx table alone was beyond the capacity of my strength but now that it was heavily laden with vases filled with flowers it was not to be considered. To move it would be to break the vases and my mind's ears seemed to hear in advance the crash that would arouse the "dragon" (nurse) and what a time I would have explaining to her!

Thus hesitating I remained in bed in a semi-reclining position, resting on one elbow, looking hopelessly toward the table and then at the face of the sleeping nurse, whom I could not see very well. The sound of her deep, regular breathing, however, was more reassuring than the sight of her face would have been.

Reluctantly obeying a force that was stronger than

my inclination to disobey, I arose cautiously creeping on tiptoe to the table with fear and trembling for the lives of my vases and thinking of the humiliation to myself when the nurse should arise in the execution of her duty.

I stood for a moment beside the table, tears welling up into my eyes at the tyranny of a force that not only compelled me to attempt the impossible but to destroy my treasured vases which held the fragrant offering that had come to gladden my tired senses. While thus hesitating, I could feel the force pressing me, very pronouncedly, bearing heavily upon me, pushing me nearer and nearer the table until I touched it with my body. Then in the desperation of accepting the inevitable, I placed both hands upon its sides, testing it for the safest and most effective hold. To my surprise as well as relief, it lifted lightly and floated gently to the bedside without disarranging as much as a rose, leaving me standing in amazement just where I had stood when I placed my hands upon it, and too much relieved that no harm had come to the vases to fully appreciate the wonder of the performance.

After standing in petrified amazement for some minutes with my eyes fixed upon the table, I slowly walked over and again stood by it and being very, weak, put one hand on it to steady myself, but quickly removed it, as there was a distinct shock as of electricity, which caused me to refrain from further direct contact with it.

A voice came in a tone deep with seriousness:

"Choose a red rose and white one—the red one you will hold in your right hand, the white in your left." This I did and the voice commanded, "Now get into bed."

Obedience was never one of my virtues, even as a child, and I resented its exactions upon any circumstances, therefore, I got into the bed slowly, deliberately, arranging my pillows with exaggerated precision despite the roses in my hands, feeling that I should be requested to do these things, not commanded. Finally I lay down with a red rose crushed in my right hand and a white one in my left, wondering what would be the next requirement or what would be the outcome of what the night had already required.

I was so weak and tired that I did not prognosticate very long as I felt sleep coming gently down and shutting out all perplexities. This condition was instantly and most effectively relieved by the calm announcement:

"You are going to petrify tonight."

"What?" I cried in alarm, echoing "Petrify?" but no further explanation was vouchsafed.

"What did you say?" I called again and again into the unresponsive blackness, and even while I listened a coldness began creeping upon me and continued ever increasing until I felt that I was freezing.

I did everything I could to shake it off, feeling that I was a victim of suggestion. I told myself in all seriousness that I was not cold at all but was instead comfortably warm and honestly tried to feel myself so, even when the sense of coldness became so intense that to deny it was unreasonable. I could have cried out for cover though the night was hot, with a sultry threatening of rain in the atmosphere and not a breath of air stirring.

I looked about the room but the semi-darkness showed it to be normal except for a frosty mist that was hanging about with a bluish light scintillating and spreading itself in pale illumination. The table stood beside the bed and as if to reassure myself—to prove its presence—I reached out my hand, still retaining the rose, and took a piece of fern that lay loosely upon it and pressed it into my hair, which was rather loose and disheveled about my face, as my hair generally is at night (I like to sleep with it unconfined). I do not remember that I had any defined motive in the act unless it was the subconscious desire for material confirmation of that which was in the act of transpiring.

A moment later I could move neither hand nor foot, could not move a muscle in my body as it became rigid, the eyes wide open and the power of speech gone. I think I must have been rather terrified or distressed for an instant, for I remember the impulse of tearing myself away from it, which gradually gave place to resignation and observation.

The very atmosphere in the room seemed electrified, alive, and out of its quivering vibrations came the form of my mother, who stood by the bedside looking down upon me lovingly and tenderly with great illuminated eyes. She wore a gray dressing gown, which I recognized as the one she had worn when last I saw her in the earth life. In her hand she held a gorgeous white flower, stretching it toward me, almost touching my face with it. The fragrance seemed to fill the entire room, neutralizing, overpowering that of the earth flowers, and my mood blended into the perfect harmony of the offering. I wanted to reach out and take the flower from her but conscious of the impotency of my hand, manacled by some strange power, I could only glance at it as it lay out from me showing tiny glimpses of crushed red petals between the clasped fingers. So life-like did she seem that the impulse was strong upon me to kiss her and tell her how glad I was that she had come, but this being impossible, I cried out mentally:

"Mama—little mama—speak to me."

"The body is to the soul what the flower is to the fragrance," she whispered softly and smilingly, and then slowly faded away while still I was looking at the place where she had stood, my soul calling to her to come back, though the cold was stiffening my body and freezing my blood. Then I fell to wondering if clothes and flowers really have souls that pass into other realms, and are these still the possessions of those who owned them in the earth life—do they have souls at all? Was there really no end to perplexing problems to press in upon one from every side? My attention was diverted by Meon standing before me, plainer and more illuminated than I ever had seen him before. I called out to him:

"Meon, what is the matter—am I dying?"

He looked into my eyes steadily and ignoring my question said impressively:

"Truth stands unveiled before thee—let it not pass unobserved," and with his steady gaze upon me, resistence and perplexities gave way and I began trying to analyze my predicament as the cold waves, like a rising tide, every surge of which was perceptible, ebbed nearer and nearer life's centre. Then, as it were, I felt them touch, and stiffened as the full tide of insensibility enveloped me physically while mentally I grew proportionately more active and discerning. I could no longer see Meon but felt that he was near, still looking at me with sternness in his eyes and command in his attitude, impelling me to a discernment that, inferring from his words and attitude was very essential. Then I felt myself to be absolutely alone, alone with the mystery of myself, the roses and the cold.

Suddenly I was conscious of the most compelling sensation I ever felt—*I* was a thing apart from the cold, frozen body which seemed a heavy wall surrounding me as though I were wrapped in something cold and heavy. I realized an independence of it, an existence without it, and half resented it as a thing that bound me, that interfered with my freedom. As I acknowledged this to myself, the *I* principle or inner strength grew in power until it seemed to reach out beyond the cold, useless exterior and meet, in a cooperative sense, a greater strength or power. I could feel the two meeting, touching, as it were, through the dead coldness of the physical body which had become as nothing. Then came the gradual birth of a grand sensation—a merging of the strength within and that without, blending, powerful in its cooperation. I felt that this great new power was mine, mine to use as I elected, mine to draw upon at will.

A few seconds later I perceived that the physical body was moving and *I* within it, as a thing apart, was being lifted by the cooperative strength of this *within* and *without* power. The body was as insensible as a stone with a stone's cold heaviness, but it moved lightly up, up, slowly, cautiously, until within a few inches of the ceiling where it stopped. While it was thus suspended this outer and inner strength came together more pronouncedly and forcibly, as if to further define and cement their oneness of power in independence of the body.

Then the *I*, the ego, looked with analysis upon its relationship with its physical environment of which it had always deemed itself a part, or rather a *whole,* and came to the conclusion that the soul and body are two separate entities, that the soul is independent of the body and uses it only for the convenience of functioning while in the earth life. The body is only moulded clay—the soul or spirit is the *real* life, the life everlasting.

When this conviction was full upon me a voice came crying joyously:

"It is well—it is well," and many spirits joined in the demonstrations of rejoicing that I had not permitted this "unveiled truth to pass unobserved," and a great exultation possessed me as the body was gently lowered on the bed, head on pillow, more perfectly adjusted than before the ascent. It is impossible to convey any idea of a condition so out of harmony with the automatic or involuntary actions of physical life but suffice it to say, it was wonderful, this drawing the line between soul and body, defining it, feeling that the soul recognizes not only itself but a cooperative relationship too new and mysterious to be either fully understood or explained. Veritably it seemed to recognize itself as a part of God—one with all power.

Then slowly the cold began giving away to warm comfortable life, to the accompaniment of a prickling stinging sensation not unlike when one's "foot goes to sleep."

My body was miserably stiff and uncomfortable as sensibility returned, but I was so tired that although the dawn had come, I drifted into the slumber that consumes weariness, the chilly memory of the night being obliterated for the time being.

Long after sunrise when I opened my eyes there were the material footprints—the flower-laden table sat beside the bed, in my right hand was a crushed rose of red, in my left one of white and a sprig of fern was tangled in my hair.

CHAPTER XIII.

VISIONS. LOVE SPIRITUALIZED BY DEATH.

The nurse looked upon the table and at me with interrogatory disapproval, which I feigned not to see, closing my eyes to avoid her questioning when she picked up the fern and crushed roses from the floor where I had tossed them. I shrank from the sound of a human voice—in fact, any sound was almost painful to me, I was in such a sensitive, spiritualized condition, feeling more than ever a creature of another world.

The day was well into the afternoon before this super-sensitiveness gave way to normality, and I went into the bath almost free from it.

While I bathed a voice came speaking hurriedly, as though explaining something.

"What are you saying?" I asked, listening more intently.

Then followed an explanation concerning the construction of an electrical appliance for heating water and heating rooms generally, to which I replied:

"You must know that I understand little of the practical application of electricity."

"But why not learn it? The knowledge of its *real* value is in its infancy."

"I may—some day," I replied almost indifferently, without realizing that my indifference was an offense to one so deeply in earnest, and felt a tinge of self-condemnation when a moment later a retreating voice wafted back with reproach in its tone—"Oh, if people only understood what they call *electricity*—the pos-

The Dead Are Alive

sibilities of it." I wished that I had listened more discriminatingly, as by my indifference, I doubtless forfeited a truth which otherwise might have been given me. All afternoon I could not forget it and kept wondering to what extent things exist in the invisible world before they are manifested in this and such kindred conjectures. Possibly the recognition of this point—that things *do* exist in the other world before they do in this—was the object sought—who knows?

When night came I was glad, as I was weak and weary almost to unconsciousness, and invited sleep with something of a longing for it. But it did not come. Instead I lay wide awake thinking in a listless, undefined way, with my consciousness closed to the invisible world, counting every stroke of the clock as it chimed out on the soft stillness of the night, which held my soul en rapport with its mood. When twelve struck I remember there was a pleasing sensation that when it struck again its sound would be reduced to the minimum.

Distrait, with eyes wide open, staring into the semi-darkness, I could sense a change coming over the room and discern a slowly gathering mist, which became so pronounced that it obscured the walls and objects in the room. Then it began growing in scope until it became boundless in expanse, lights and colors mingling and intermingling in it. Then it took on the look of the sea, as though it were, in fact, water; showing the inhabitants of the sea, "those under the crust of her roof and those above it," exercising a potent, invisible power which will not always remain beyond the range of our conception. There were ships* that traveled with even more fleetness and sureness of purpose "under the crust of her roof" than those above it. A terrible blackness, as of a storm, yet not a storm, was upon the sea destroying the ships that rode upon her waves without injury to those that plied beneath them. Then there was a calm sea with ships passing down beneath the waves easily and unperturbed; others, differently made, passed serenely, high above the sea in the air, and there was something ominous about it. Then a change came over the scene and when the white mist showed again there was a darkness within it, which I perceived represented land with its cities, rivers, lakes, trees and flowers. There were the inhabitants, those on the earth and those in the air about and above it, in appearance so like that it was difficult to distinguish one kind from the other except for the positions maintained. Then came soldiers of all nations in full uniform and war equipment, flags flying, marching, marching, ever marching toward an illusive goal which was labeled "PEACE," and like a will-o-the-wisp it moved ever before them as they grimly pursued it with the attitude of "We will have peace if we have to fight for it." And while "peace" was yet afar off, they marched with the sound as though they waded in mud—but it was not mud, it was blood—they were wading in it, splashing it over everything. I turned away to shut out the horrible sight and sound, and when I looked again—but I will not attempt to describe the desolation of the readjustment. I turned from it and its long drawn out agony, and had not the courage to look back for some time. When I did a change was over everything—the whole world

---

*Publisher's Note: The following was written in 1913, before the outbreak of the European war.

seemed transformed in every way—a wonderful event had come and unity was established among the people who were rejoicing exceedingly. Suddenly the water mists and the land mists formed themselves into a gigantic map of the world, and the people, as one great family, were within it, while on the line of the circumference the word "PEACE" came out in large, illuminated letters, which moved like living things around the map and then formed themselves across the diameter, embracing the whole world. Slowly the scene began fading, the map going first, then the people, then the letters one by one. As my tired eyes were riveted upon them in the darkness, over and about was a halo, dim but discernible, which manifested itself in a scintillating way. Then the scenes slowly gave way and I was looking at the familiar paper on the wall and the picture just as naturally as though there had been no intrusion of that which was non-existent. There was a sense of relief when I looked out of the window and saw the reflection of the street lamp and listened to the street noises, trying to shake off the "coming shadows" of something terrible that was nagging my consciousness into apprehensiveness.

This, however, was not the only occasion on which such phenomena presented themselves but they came only when I was too weak and ill to care whether they came or not. I have tried to "call up" something of the kind at will, but so far have never succeeded. Of course, they are only visions and may or may not have a meaning; but strange as it may seem, from the very beginning of these manifestations I have resented the *vision* phase of it. Even now it almost irritates me to write about them. I have in mind an especially irritating incident—one afternoon flags of the different nations waved, going up and coming down, changing positions, uninterruptedly for hours as plainly as though they really existed and had some meaning in their activity. This persisted until I felt as though I could fight every country that ever had a flag, so tired of them did I become. Scenery, lakes, seas, flowers, trees, beauteous creatures, have come and gone, ever changing, in the meshes of the mist—veritable dream pictures of loveliness to which I did not especially object, although I did not encourage them. Be that as it may, that which I saw I wanted to have at least a semblance of existence, a pretension anyway.

The next morning after the first "attack of visions," I was thoroughly displeased with myself and felt more strongly than ever the advisability of tearing myself away from the domination of this tyrannical mystery which had held me for days, if not entirely against my will, certainly against my judgment. I was determined to end it all by getting out of bed that very day. The irony of such a determination when one is almost too weak to lift one's hands! But something had to be done—just to think I had at one "sitting" seen what seemed like the world as a giant battlefield, in all its bloody horrors; then a valley of desolation, in the tragedy of readjustment, all of which was finally "swallowed up" by the victory of unity—of UNIVERSAL PEACE, a kind of paradise on earth. It impressed me more than I would care to admit even now, the temptation to interpret it was ever recurring to me and it seemed that I could forsee awful things. Then I would try to persuade myself that it had no meaning and when it persisted I could only take consolation in feeling that

"Time is the old justice that examines all offenders," and time would tell.*

While I grappled with the "vision" problem a telephone message came announcing the arrival in the city of a little nephew, whom I welcomed as a

---

FOOT NOTE—(Written January, 1916.)
*While it was during the summer of 1911 that this series of manifestations presented itself it was nearly two years before I put it in manuscript form and not until September, 1913, that I first made an effort to interest a publisher in it. At that time a world's war seemed such a remote possibility that publishers were not inclined to risk it—to say nothing of the subject matter of the book in general. After several unsuccessful efforts at publication I finally modified the "war visions," changing them from well defined outlines into the general form in which they remain. I then continued taxing publishers with the manuscript until the war materialized when I put it regretfully aside, as a thing that had failed, and tried to forget it. But now that the war comes nearer the end, perhaps a pre-vision as to its outcome might be of interest At any rate I find myself restless under a re-awakened desire to have it published.

The manifestations were generally heralded by the assembling of the flags of the nations. That of Germany came first and others would come floating in, one by one, and all would wave about, intermingling, until they became a conglomerated mass from which they would finally emerge stained by a redness as of blood, rendering some almost indistinguishable—notably that of Austria. The United States always came in toward the end, emerging with only a few drops of blood, therefore, I should say that when the United States loses that few drops of blood the end of the war will not be far off.

The readjustment will last for some time and be almost as demoralizing as the war,—a veritable commercial war, with the revolutionary spirit stalking relentlessly in more countries than one.

To the Allies will be the victory in the present war. An emperor will die before the end. There will be many deaths in high places. Many fires—one great one, as of a city burning. Austria's throne will become vacant—Hungary will become a separate nation. Russia will gain, comparatively, more than any other nation in every way; the United States in wealth, as it will practically rehabilitate all Europe. The French soldier will go down in history as the bravest and best, the German, the most relentless. Italy is serving her double purpose splendidly, the religious significance of which is patent only to those who care to be observant. Germany will not by any means be annihilated but will be our next important Republic. The fall of Turkey is inevitable.

And England? England will come in on the "home run"—and will not be found wanting on land or sea.

In the process of readjustment India and Ireland, after a time, will have home rule.

There is a reason for all things and the purpose of this war is to settle for *all times* national differences and "clean the slate" for the new dispensation that is being ushered in—a new world is being born—but there will be no settling down until all national differences are adjusted. Then a world's teacher will come amongst us as the new dispensation is recognized and ushered in, in peace and universal brotherhood.

needed diversion. He was the child of my younger brother, whose wife had died a short time before. While I was very fond of the mother I had never seen the child, who was then about two years old. While I appreciated the courtesy I was somewhat surprised to have the wife's parents bring the child to visit me as I had never met either of them.

A few minutes later they were ushered in, and introductions over, the grandfather placed the child on the bed beside me saying:

"And this is your brother's boy."

He was a pretty, intellectual child, with golden curls and large, expressive brown eyes that looked questioningly into mine. I put my arms about him without any intention of kissing him but suddenly I felt an intense desire to do so and asked him if he was not going to kiss me. He seemed not quite sure about it but after a moment's deliberation, bent his little curly head and touched my mouth with his rosebud lips. I released him so his grandfather might take him if he so desired, fearing he might fall if not restrained by more force than was mine to exercise. I was astonished to hear quite plainly a voice cry out:

"Oh, Fanny, hold him again—I want to kiss him."

And there standing beside the bed, in broad daylight, leaning lovingly over her baby, was its little mother, just as lifelike as I had ever seen her!

Again I folded the child within my arms and as I did so I could distinctly feel her arms about mine and hear her faint love-laden whisper:

"Oh, my baby—my little boy."

Pulling his face down to mine I again kissed it but this time I felt distinctly a cold obstruction between the child's lips and mine, as its mother's invisible arms about mine held it tightly clasped to my breast. At that moment I felt what a sacred, holy thing a mother's love is—it passed through my entire being and held me glorified, uplifted—the purest passion that ever flooded my soul. Suddenly the pressure lifted, leaving me almost unconscious with weakness. The divine spark of motherhood, with its illuminating joy, which had been loaned me for that brief instant, had gone, possibly never to return. Yet, I feel that I shall always know what a love of a mother is like—a mother's love spiritualized by death —a deathless love.

When released, the child sat looking at me in a puzzled way—who can say, child though he was, that his mother's love did not touch his consciousness? His grandfather came and stood by the bedside, unconsciously falling under the influence of his dead child who stood so near him, "the substance of things hoped for, the evidence of things unseen." Looking at the child and then at me, he said with a tremor in his voice:

"So like her."

"Yes," I echoed, "so like *her*."

After removing the child, he looked at me and said with solicitude:

"How tired and ill you look—I hope the boy has not overtaxed your strength."

"Not in the least," I assured him, in a mumbling sort of way, as talking was rather difficult for my lips had a sense of deadness caused by conveying a kiss over the span that divides life and death. Therefore, I closed my eyes to avoid further conversation until I was equal to it. A gentle voice which I remembered so well, came like a caress:

"Thank you, dear, it was for this I had them bring him. I wish I could thank them, too."

"I will do it for you," I promised. "Thank you," came the voice so weak that it was scarcely audible, but she did not go away. Instead, she remained in the room the greater part of the day near her baby. I could feel her presence and on several occasions caught the faintest glimpses of her but she did not again converse with me nor did she materialize.

Subconsciously these dear "old folks" had acted in accordance with a request from the world invisible, by making a journey to take a baby to a sick aunt who had never seen him, that his dead mother might avail herself of the occasion to hold her baby in her arms and kiss him, while the divine current of her love flowed like a benediction over his little body.

> "There is no death! the stars go down,
> To rise on some fairer shore,
> And bright in Heaven's jeweled crown
> They shine forever more.
> And ever near us, though unseen,
> The dear, immortal spirits tread,
> For all the boundless universe
> Is life—there is no dead."

How I wanted to tell this dear old couple that the child they mourned as dead stood beside them radiantly happy, bathing them doubly in her purified love because of their tender care of her child.

CHAPTER XIV.

BACK ACROSS THE DARK SPAN.

The psychology of a love so beautiful remained with and haunted me far into the night, as I lay looking listlessly out of the window on the moonlight —just a waking dreaminess wrapped in careless, contented indifference, which a peaceful joyousness sometimes imparts.

It was nearing midnight before I drifted into a sleep from which I was rudely awakened by a loud knocking, which became ever louder and more pronounced. I sat up quickly, staring inquiringly in the direction from whence it came. As the noise came from the direction parallel to my head I was obliged to turn around as well as to sit up in order to see what it was. So numerous had been my surprises during the previous weeks that I had come to regard myself as being immune from surprise and I now realized that I had grievously erred in this, as I stared in surprise and horror at the very last thing that one would ever expect to see coming back across the dark span!

Moving serenely up and down, using a large white pedestal on which was a life-size statue of Sapho as a background for its manipulations—was a crutch! It continued to move up and down methodically, becoming plainer and plainer, until the hand manipulating it could be seen distinctly—a hand so characteristic as to be recognizable among thousands— that of my father. A crutch had made his life on earth a "long, sad requiem," and there before me was the evidence that it had pursued him even into eternity! My fondness for my father made the contemplation of this thing a horror beyond expression. With heart beating wildly, my eyes riveted on it, in anguish I cried out:

"Oh, papa is it you—really you?"

"Yes, child, it is I," came the placid answer, as the crutch disappeared and I perceived him coming nearer, and asked in an awed whisper:

"Are you crippled in that life, too?"

"Why no—I am a veritable giant of strength and vigor," he replied, easily, as he took my arm with a grip that verified his assertion.

"But why did you bring that hateful thing?"

"That you might know it is I."

"I should have known anyway."

"Possibly; but do not believe *all* that you see and hear from this side—there are many deceivers."

"Deceivers?" I echoed in alarm.

"Yes; unhappy creatures near the earth, who, to attract and maintain the attention and consideration of those with whom they can communicate, make the most preposterous representations."

"How shocking—but how is one to guard against them?"

"One soon learns to discriminate; 'like attracts like,' and by keeping your spirit pure only the highest can come into spirit communion with you."

So intense had been my interest as I listened that I did not realize that I was still sitting in a cramped position, with my feet crossed under me. He seemed pleased and said, "You used to sit that way nearly all the time when you were a little girl," and helped to smooth out the pillow as I lay back on it in joyous readiness for a tete-a-tete with the idol of my childhood, coaxing eagerly:

"Now, papa, dear, tell me everything—how you came and all about it."

"Coming was easy enough, but to get you to hear and understand was quite a different matter. Often I have come to you, called and caressed you, but when you heeded me not I would go away sorrowing deeply that my little girl refused to turn her face to the light."

"I am glad I can see you now—glad to know you still live and love me."

"There is no death—it is all a beautiful birth as the people of earth will soon recognize."

"Tell me all about it," I said with finality, expecting to have the whole story in a nutshell—all the mysteries solved at once.

"The earth life well lived is one of the most important phases of existence and means much in those that are yet to come."

"Are there more than one?" I asked in astonishment.

"It is well that one is not all."

"How many are there?"

"I have yet to learn. You know I came here bound by the traditional beliefs and have been about as busy unlearning as I have learning."

"Are things so different?"

"In so far as *everlasting* punishment and a *localized* Hell and Heaven are concerned, yes; but we must not discuss such things, let's talk about children, as I have not long to remain."

"Very well, papa," I assented, trying to suppress my disappointment that he had so abruptly changed the subject most interesting to me. After speaking with loving solicitude of each of his children, calling them by name, he turned away saying:

"I must go now."

"No—not so soon," I protested. "There are many things I want you to explain to me."

"Create today thy life for tomorrow. I must go, as there are requirements in this existence just as there are in the earth life."

When I realized that he was really going I called after him, "Oh, Papa, tell me—am I going to die?"

"There is much you will be given to know—be patient, very patient—goodbye."

"But, Papa, you did not tell me—am I going to die?" I called after him in the darkness but no answering voice came and I knew for a certainty he had gone. I sat up in bed again and looked around where I had seen the crutch, half afraid that I would see it again but there was nothing that even suggested the supernatural except a chillness which caused me to shiver slightly and put the sheet up over me as I lay down again.

On the following evening when my fiance came I wanted so much to tell him of the scene with the baby the day before and the crutch of the previous night but when I realized that I must not, my heart ached at the "rift in the lute" this secretiveness on my part was causing in the perfect harmony of our love— just a little minor discord, but it was ever there. While frankness may be dangerous waters for the sailing of ships of State, the same can be said of the lack of it in the paddling of Cupid's canoe.

After he had read aloud to me for some time I felt less the oppression of my enforced lack of candor and enjoyed listening to a story of life instead of death, such as I had listened to for many weeks.

After the story was concluded, on my natural impulse of frankness, I did a very foolish thing—I attempted to tell him about the crutch that I had seen manipulating beside the white pedestal. The nurse looked shocked and he looked at me in undisguised disapproval and disappointment, saying:

"And I was congratulating myself that you were better!"

"I am all right, sir," I assured him but this was too much for his toleration. He left the house thoroughly discouraged and no doubt disgusted, while I lay dampening the pillow with the tears I could not restrain, listening to his footsteps as he went down the stairs. I next heard the gate latch click and knew he was gone.

The next day, to my utter bereavement, every statue, pedestal and almost every movable thing was taken out of the room, leaving it not only without a background for ghostly manipulations but so desolate in appearance that these words kept running ceaselessly through my brain:

> "Bare ruined choirs where late the sweet birds sang."

CHAPTER XV.

WRITING.

When the nurse told me the doctor considered the room "more sanitary when less crowded," I made no comment but simply turned my head to the foot of the bed so my eyes would not continually rest upon the devastation of what I considered the most beautiful room in the world at a time when I needed its beauty most—another dagger tipped with the poison of mistaken kindness!

As the afternoon wore on I became more and more restless and dissatisfied and had to battle with myself to keep from being really angry at such presumption but my "promise of faithfulness" embraced *self-control* and I strove to be equal to the test put upon it. Nor was it as easy as it sounds. I resolutely shut out the voices of the invisibles and looked out with my thoughts on the gathering storm. The black clouds, the lightning flashes and the thunder made me wish the wind would blow and the rain would come down in torrents to harmonize with my mood, to say nothing of dispelling the sultriness of the atmosphere. After some time of this depression I felt that I must do something—anything—to counteract it. With this end in view I asked the nurse to bring me writing materials and when she did so and made me comfortable by extra pillows I began writing letters.

Before proceeding very far I perceived that my pencil did not respond to my mental direction with the usual swiftness and accuracy but I charged it to my weakness and tried to continue. The pencil was lifted from the paper in the middle of a word and almost removed from my hand. I began again but it was pulled at, touched, shaken and lifted with such persistence that at last I gave up writing as the letters were not of such importance that they had to be executed under such stress. Thus arguing I lay back disgusted, with the pencil relaxed between my fingers. No sooner had I done so than a numbness, as of something coming down into my arm and permeating it, was distinctly felt, rendering the arm and hand utterly useless. This I regarded very seriously, as fear of paralysis was upon me; but thoroughly alarmed as I was there was something that pressed against removing the hand from the position in which it was, and I could only regard it apprehensively. Then I saw the hand vibrating and the pencil, independent of my direction, assume a writing position and, propelled by a force and guided by an intelligence outside of my own, began *writing,* yes, writing with my own hand yet I did not know what it was until I read it. How wonderful it seemed and "still the wonder grew" when I discovered some of the writing was in a language I did not understand!

Then the rain came down torrentially, lightning flashed, thunder rolled and the wind blew wildly, but heeding them not I wrote on and on, enchanted by this weird and marvelous manifestation. Held in bondage by an intelligence that was dominating its every movement independently, my hand gave some wonderful demonstrations of what could be accomplished in this way. There were communications from friends and loved ones, predictions (a world's war amongst them) thoughts, poems, etcetera.

I here reproduce one of the poems which was given that afternoon wherein the soul and body are treated as two separate entities, defining their relationship, as it were.

THE CASTLE ME

I dwell in the Castle Me
    Where I would reign alone
But Good and Evil are here
    Beside me on the throne.

I gaze out of its windows
    See it lashed by life's sea
While I grow ever stronger
    Within the Castle Me.

But some day I'll go away
    And leave it here below
For I'll no longer need it
    In the realms where I go.

Earth will take it back again
    And dust with dust remould
Just as tho' it had never
    Harbored a human soul.

While I go on my journey
    Unto regions of light
Where there'll be no sorrowing
    And there will come no night.

Now re-read it as I did and the fullness of its meaning will come upon you bringing a sense of *soul*—independence of the body—a recognition of the ego, as a thing apart from the body and yet manifesting within it.

This wonderful ability to write—to pass my hand into the realm of the Invisible and bring back ofttimes strange and startling records, still remains with me but I rarely exercise it—what is the use? Even as I write this book I constantly combat efforts of invisible intelligences to control my pen and incorporate their views in the writing thereof, but, as it is a record of my personal experiences, I am recording it incident by incident just as it came to me, regardless of how it may sound or seem; therefore, I repel such interferences.

Using the pencil was not the only phase of this independent writing that manifested itself through me. On numerous occasions invisible hands have taken mine and with my index finger written on walls, doors, portieres, bed or anything convenient—even on my lap. Where there was no visible result each word was spelled out slowly, letter by letter, as my mind accepted and retained it. If for any reason a letter was obscure or I failed to grasp it, it was immediately rewritten until correctly conveyed.

At first all writings were accomplished by pronounced vibrations of the hand but gradually this ceased and the hand appeared practically normal.

While admitting this form of writing to be one of the most wonderful phases of my psychological experiences, I strongly advise against indulging in it indiscriminately or in the spirit of levity. When the hand is passed into the Beyond it is generally taken by any presence that happens to be near and if levity attracts irresponsible beings, in accordance with the law of "like attracts like" the result is as often misleading as otherwise. There are entities in the world of shadows who do not hesitate to give the most astounding untruths just as there are on earth. This I have proved to my own satisfaction and hence this is a subject that should be approached only when one is mentally and spiritually en rapport with the highest influences—bathed in purity of purpose and strength of soul more powerful than adverse influences can possibly be always remembering where Good rules evil is powerless. Unless we have some affinity for evil it cannot touch us, therefore, when any experiment is undertaken with our thoughts "in the right key" we lessen the chances of forming undesirable invisible acquaintances which are really of more importance than visibles. *Our thoughts should be carefully trained in the right channel before attempting any experiments at all, and then only with careful discrimination.*

"You can never tell what your thoughts will do
    In bringing you hate or love,
For thoughts are things and their airy wings
    Are swifter than carrier dove.

They follow the law of the universe
    Each thing must create its kind,
And they speed o'er the track to bring you back
    Whatever went out from your mind."

That "thoughts are things" cannot be overlooked in the study of psychology—one might say it is the keynote—it is by *thought* we converse with the soul world—our thoughts in the spirit world are very much what our personal appearance is in the earth life, only more so. Our invisible associates are very much what our inner thoughts are as that is what attracts them.

All that stormy afternoon was consumed in watching my benumbed hand and arm serving accurately and swiftly an intelligence other than mine and looking at the result with as much surprise and wonderment as if executed by the hand of another.

When the sun was set and the evening shadows came into the room the nurse suggested that I must be very tired and insisted on putting the writing material away and sending the letters to be mailed, to which I replied "they are unfinished" and carefully folded what I had written and put it in an envelope, placed it in the box and handed it to her to put on my desk, which she did without comment.

Then the night came on, dark with continuous rain and a distinct coolness in the atmosphere but there was no sleep as it was *Tuesday* night and I could not tear myself away from the watching and waiting it fastened upon me. How weary I felt of waiting, weary of life, even weary of the promise of death. All night long my consciousness was open to the silence—I called into it but no answering voice came —the only form of communication was a mingling mass of letters which arranged and rearranged themselves in a meaningless way before my eyes, continuously vibrating, as I tried and tried to decipher them. Hands would take mine and write words or letters indiscriminately on the bed covers with my first finger. This continued until in very desperation I closed my eyes, feeling that I would despise writing unto the end of time; would never try to decipher any more such communications; never again permit my hand to be used for such purposes. This resentful and rebellious mood lasted until day had almost come and as I felt it giving way opened my eyes and was almost shocked to see those vibrating, tantalizing letters in the identical position I had last seen them. I viewed them almost indifferently now, feeling that it did not matter whether they were there or not, then in a gentle, methodical way, the vibrating letters formed themselves into this sentence: "This is thy lesson in patience—be thou patient even unto the end." And thus another Tuesday night took its place in the file of yesterdays.

CHAPTER XVI.

SOUL AND BODY IN PROCESS OF SEPARATION.

"There is a natural body and there is a spiritual body."—St. Paul.

The next day found me so weak and weary that I mentally protested against the least exertion, even the bath, my one diversion, but the echo that came back, "I will be faithful," compelled my compliance according to my promise. I protested in a subconscious way, just as I did about breathing or any other exertion, voluntary or involuntary. I was tired of it all—the endless tragedy of it!

As I went into the bath room I stopped and leaned against the door facing to rest and almost succumbed to the temptation to turn back to the bed, regardless of the invisible world and its requirements. Again I seemed to hear myself saying: "I will be faithful," which spurred me on until I stood beside the tub. With one foot poised in mid air I stood transfixed, looking with wide, amazed eyes at *myself* stretched full length in the tub!

My foot slowly descended to the floor as a sensation of awe came upon me. There was no mistaking it—there I lay—there I stood—one *I* gazing at the other. Common courtesy not to mention physical impossibilities forbade me joining my "other self" in the bath; beside which I did not care to annihilate that "other self" without giving it an opportunity of explaining why I had waited so late in life to become twins!

While watching it eagerly it began evidencing life, vibrating, splashing about as tho' in reality taking a bath—the thing was awesome and I trembled somewhat as I looked at it—it was certainly *me* and there *I* stood looking at it, watching it manifest life, and acting as I would act. Then almost suddenly *it* became dual as it struggled in the water—distinctly I could see another body, shadowy but defined, an exact duplicate, confined within the physical body, the duplicate as distinctly discernible as the original. This body interpenetrated the physical, the relation of the physical body to it being very much that of a glove covering the hand, the inner body directing the movements of the outer body as the hand directs the glove. At first the duplicate or shadow body used its potency in regulating the movements of the physical body, then it seemed to withdraw within itself, letting go of the physical body, as it were, which became heavily still. Independently of the outer the inner body began slightly vibrating, more and more pronouncedly and with ever increasing power.

In the exercise of its movements, now unhampered by the physical, it began pulling up the feet with that peculiar vibratory motion so characteristic of these manifestations and continued pulling until the "shadow" feet came up to about midway between the knees and ankles only to fall back and vibrate up again and again. Then the "shadow" hands began jerking and pulling themselves up loosening them, as it were, from the physical hands that lay still and motionless. They did not succeed so well as the feet; with the greatest apparent effort they could come no higher than just about the wrists. Then the "shadow" hands and feet began working at the same time and the entire inner body moved in apparent readjustment—the hands and feet repeatedly pulling up to what seemed their limit only to fall back and start all over again while the physical body lay white and still in the water.

It is impossible to conceive of how fascinating and awe-inspiring this phenomenon was—it held me oblivious to all things else. It was evident that the spirit or soul body was trying to force itself out of the physical—trying to gain strength by drawing up the hands and feet to propel it in an upward direction beyond the physical confines. The "shadow" head was pressing hard against the cranium but never one time did it go for even the faintest fraction beyond. The "shadow" eyes pulled away from their physical windows, the nose and ears drew away, but the mouth remained firm. I realized that I was being shown the modus operandi of the separation of the soul from the body and truly it was a grewsomely wonderful thing to look upon.

So engrossed was I in its contemplation that I took no note of time and just when it promised a revelation of the exit, a voice so startled me I nearly jumped into the tub amid the strange, weird dissection.

"You have been in here quite long enough," and punctuating her words with her presence the nurse stood looking at me, her face mirroring her surprise and annoyance to find I had not even been in the water. Suppressing her annoyance she said, with forced solicitude:

"How stupid of me to permit you to remain so long—come into bed at once."

So saying she took my cold hand and half leaning

on her I went into bed with a heart heavy with disappointment, feeling that but for ill-timed interruption, my eyes would have feasted upon the mystery of mysteries—the goodbye scene between the soul and its earth abode.

With half closed eyes I listened without hearing her lecture on "Taking the proper care of oneself." Then I heard her go into the bath room and turn out the water, wondering vaguely if the apparition was still there, yet realizing that even if it were the power to see it was not hers. Strange that one person can see such things and another cannot! Yet such is a truth that can be demonstrated.

When she came in she brought some wine and tried to cheer me but my disappointment was too poignant to be dissipated by mere wine and words, especially as her promises were for physical betterment of which I never expected to avail myself, for death seemed in a measure to have already foreclosed its mortgage on me.

What I had seen haunted me; it seemed my mind had photographed it; wherever I looked I seemed to see that weird, struggling spirit in its desperate efforts to escape from the prison house of flesh in which it was incarcerated. Shutting my eyes did not shut it out but rather intensified it. In fancy I almost felt a "shadow" body struggling within me. I knew it must be there but was it really struggling to escape? I was sure it was, but why did it struggle when I was so willing that it should escape?

I think there must have been something of exultation in the knowledge that now I could answer that oft-repeated question—"Where is the soul?" to which everybody seems to have some kind of answer, theory or conjecture, but which inevitably reverts to the agnostic admission, "I do not know." And *now* I did *know* and the knowledge was wonderfully uplifting spiritually.

This relationship of soul and body can be likened unto the interpenetration of water poured on sand. The water sinks into the earth, fertilizes, gives it life and the ability to reproduce and yet it is not visible to the physical eye any more than is the soul in the human earth. Water is the soul of mother earth—spirit the soul of human earth. Water goes back from whence it came—so does the spirit—each in its own way by its own process.

When night and the magic of its stillness was upon everything it all came back and the "shadow" body within was calling to other "shadows" that had been released from their prisons of flesh and they came renewing the promise of my release and we all rejoiced together. My body had become a thing apart and I no longer included it in thought of myself—it was now a useless thing from which I would soon escape.

Then in a sense of humility, I wondered why this wonderful experience, this knowledge, had been given to me instead of one more spiritually worthy, to one of the many who have spent their lives in an effort to solve this great problem. The more I thought of it the more the responsibility of the knowledge weighed upon me. I could not feel that I was entitled to it and my mood grew retrospective.

As I meditated out of the files of memory came a little song, which as a child, I sang in Sunday School long ago, entitled "PASS IT ON" and insinuated itself into the thread of my thoughts as tho' it belonged there, and in the long silent watches of the night every word came back—tramping through the halls of consciousness as tho' it were a thing of today instead of belonging to the yesterdays of childhood. It made me feel that I wanted to tell the whole world what I knew and what I had seen; and in reality "pass it on" even unto the ends of the world and I felt the thrill of such a possibility. And as the dream pages turned backward—I was a child again—time had given back its toll. I could hear the old organ pealing forth its melody in the little church nestling among the cool, green trees, saw the flowers and half dilapidated grounds, the solemn gravestones (sentinels of the dead) in the distance as I looked out of the window. In the Sunday School choir with me were the same little girls with their fluffy skirts and curly hair—the same little boys with hair wet and plastered down, fumbling nervously with catechisms, stealing glances at the lessons which they had not looked at until they came; there were the same teachers with benign and kindly faces; the same organist and we were standing about her as she played, all singing:

>"Have you had a kindness shown?
>   Pass it on, Pass it on,
>'Twas not given for you alone
>   Pass it on, Pass it on,
>Let it travel down the years
>   Let it wipe another's tears
>Till in Heaven the deed appears,
>   Pass it on, Pass it on."

And thus with the present and past intermingling, half dreaming, half-waking, "Sleep, nature's soft nurse" touched me with her tender unconsciousness and I did not wake until the day had come.

That day when I went to the bath I looked eagerly, hoping that I might again see that which had so engrossed my thoughts since its appearance the day before. But it was ever so, when I expected or looked for such things they came not but waited until I was entirely "off guard" to confront me with the most unexpected and inconceivable phenomena. With disappointment I resigned myself to the most uneventful bath of the series. I could not even feel a presence near, listened but no voice came, no hands touched me—the invisible world seemed suddenly depopulated. A chilly depression made the bath as short as it was uneventful and I returned to bed with a loneliness so intense it was painful. This sudden withdrawal of the supermundane from the mundane life produces the most oppressive loneliness imaginable. However, loneliness of any kind was a new sensation to me, for my invariable answer when any one asks me if I am ever lonely, is "Yes, sometimes—for my own company—to be alone with myself." This strikes a responsive chord in some hearts, but most admit their dependence for companionship on their fellow creatures.

And now I was lonely, really bitterly lonely, my soul was crying out for companionship—how had I offended my friends of the world invisible that they had withdrawn so entirely? "Come back to me" I whispered pleadingly "come back, I am so lonely without you" but they heeded me not, and with a heavy heart, I turned my eyes to the nurse, a mundane creature, for companionship and consolation.

Noting the unhappiness in my face she was quick to respond and came to me, asking kindly:

"What is it, dear?"

"Oh, nothing—nothing. I am so tired—tired of being sick" I made answer as a downpour of tears relieved the tenseness. She answered with conventional words of consolation:

"There, there, don't cry—you will be well in a few days, you are so much better already."

I did not reply, knowing well enough that I was neither better nor worse, but in the same negative condition that I had been for days, being held there by a force desiring it and having the ability to enforce it. I felt this force and recognized it yet was compelled to take pills and medicines until the sight and effect of them almost made me really ill, for the nurse having a professional sense of duty never let a period which demanded these inflictions pass without exercising her prerogative. I submitted as uncomplainingly as possible. But this day my enforced loneliness made me feel more kindly toward her than I had done before and I entered into a conversation with her that helped fill an otherwise lonely afternoon, and found her more intellectual than I had hoped for.

But it was when the shadow of earth called *night* came down, shutting out the light of day, that the floodtide of loneliness penetrated my being. It was then I called again and again "come;" it was then my eyes searched eagerly for a sign; then that I listened anxiously for even a whisper or a tapping; listened until hope turned ashes and weariness sifted its torturing despair into my soul. I felt like holding up my hands in the darkness that pressed upon me and calling aloud to those hidden behind it to come to me again, to speak to me, but the shadows flickering past only mocked me, assuming shapes roused my hopes until the dawn came dispelling them entirely.

Nor did the day bring their return—noon gave way to afternoon with their desertion still preying upon me. I wondered how I had offended—whether I had failed in my promised "faithfulness." Out of the stillness these words came back to haunt me, "O weaver of thy freedom, be faithful"—I seemed to hear them again and felt as though I had not been as faithful as I might have been, nor did I try to justify myself. I was only sorry with a desire to make amends, yet feeling that it was too late. A vague sense of the end was upon me, and with an aching heart I waited.

The afternoon was well spent, when the nurse noting that my usual bathing hour had passed asked:

"Aren't you going to bathe today?"

"Yes, but don't turn on the water—I'll just take a shower."

And again the temptation not to bathe assailed me as I felt really unequal to it in every way. Then I reasoned that absence of him to whom I had made the promise did not absolve me from it and I felt ashamed for almost yielding to the temptation, feeling that if I could not keep my promises when left alone my faithfulness was indeed a cheap commodity. Then I resolved to be truly faithful in every promise regardless of everything. With this determination full upon me I went into the bath and turned on the water, which came with a hard, cold impact that was almost painful. Wondering at this

I reduced the supply but it came so insufficiently, that I turned it on full again but it spurted upon me with such chilling impact, that I decided, shivering, to conclude the bath, when I noted the usual appearance of the water. It was clear and sparkling, falling in ice-like formations over my body, piling up in some places, and melting as it came in contact with my warm skin. I looked at it and examined it analytically and if it wasn't ice I never saw any! While realizing how preposterous this sounds, I took it in my hand and held it between my fingers. It melted and I shivered with the coldness of it. I held the hose high over my head permitting these crystalline formations to fall over my hair and roll on my body in their cold transparent beauty while I wondered at it.

Suddenly the whole room seemed turned into a veritable crystal palace, catching and radiating all colors, soft, glistening white predominating, and still the formations fell upon me, some melting in my hair, others rolling about in icy indiscrimination—just a page from the book of fairy dreams!

Then a change came over everything—the room seemed to merge into something else; the hose had fallen from my hand, beings of the invisible, cloud-robed and frostily-white floated about, while the "choir invisible" added its harmony. Rainbows and crystals seemed intermingling in the radiant whiteness and I felt as *one* with the pure creatures that hovered about, as the "shadow" body within me, in independence of the physical environment felt stronger and more defined as a separate entity in its association with what it recognized as creatures of its kind—free from the restraint of the material.

Above all was a sense of something too great to be measured, something which to describe would be to degrade. Infinitude interpenetrated all, including *me*.

So far had I drifted out beyond the portals of the mundane that the sound of the nurse's voice was like an explosion of dynamite as she said decisively:

"Time is up. You are not strong enough to stay in long today."

And thus from "above the clouds" wrapped within the meshes of its misty veil, I fell suddenly into a cold bath tub, with the nurse bending over me with anxiety in her face.

CHAPTER XVII.

GETHSEMANE.

"The broad minded see the truth in different religions; the narrow minded see only the differences."

After my nurse assisted me into bed she remarked with emphasis:

"You are not able to take these baths and I shall insist that the doctor have them discontinued."

When I was about to remonstrate a voice whispered:

"No more are necessary," and accordingly I responded submissively:

"I shall take no more."

Evidently pleased at what she considered an easy victory, the nurse added:

"You may take them when you are better, but not while you are so weak."

She chafed my cold hands between her warm palms, which burned almost painfully. Then pulling the light covers more snugly about me, she gave me a glass of port, which I drank to the last drop enjoying its life-giving glow.

"Try to rest now," she said kindly as she went to the South window and picked up a magazine, leaving me to the joyous realization that if my soul had been stained in the past on its terrestial journey my naturalization with the ethereal forces had beautifully demonstrated that it was no longer so, and had left no doubt as to my *oneness* with them.

"And now," I told myself, "I am ready for the transition." In profound humility I thanked whatever it was that had tortured me with waiting and preparations, at which I had so often rebelled, and felt completely compensated by this one manifestation. Even now I look back on that bath as too sacred to describe in a book, the very nature of which is bound to excite differences of opinion, even in the sympathetic, to say nothing of the criticisms of those who cannot understand and the jestings of those who will not. The last class Schopenhauer must have had in mind when he said: "Naked truth is out of place before the eyes of the profane vulgar; it can only make its appearance thickly veiled."

It is easier for me to understand those who refuse to believe anything than those who believe everything blindly. To me, knowledge and faith are synonymous. I believe in *knowing* for oneself. All else is a matter of belief. While *I* know that what I am recording in these pages is true, I do not expect my readers to accept my mere statement. I do *hope*, however, that this book will impel its readers to investigate for themselves individually. The soul's relation to the invisible world is not a matter of *belief;* it is a matter of *knowledge*—one either *knows* or does *not* know. A wider or more fascinating field of research does not exist but each person must search for himself. The gate is open to all—we can enter or not just as we will.

"He who thinks with the many must often think wrong," so Shakespeare tells us and so history proves. There was a time when "the many" believed the world had four corners and the sun moved instead of the earth but this did not make the earth square nor the sun move. When Columbus announced his intention of going in search of another world which he believed beyond the seas, only a few shared his belief, while "the many" not only doubted and scoffed but denounced him as mad. Fortunately, the existence of the Western Hemisphere did not depend on whether "the many" believed in it or not. There is always a Columbus who insists on seeing for himself and thereby is convinced, thus helping the world in its evolution towards perfection. Just as surely as there is a world beyond the sea of water there is one beyond the sea of Silence. The space world, like the sea, has its inhabitants. Looking casually you cannot discover this but when once upon it, the evidence of life appears. The sea has laws that must be complied with before we can become intimate with its creatures. Calling a fish will not bring him, but a hook and line will. There is no doubt that at one time people, except those few living where the tides brought them in, did not know what the inhabitants of the sea were like. Most people do not know what the inhabitants of Space are like except the few whose consciousness is touched by the tides of other shores and there are more of these than is generally supposed. The standing army of cowards that Public Opinion makes has within its ranks those who could tell truths stranger than any fiction ever written but dare not for fear of what people might think or say.

Vanity intrudes itself even at death. As I lay with eyes closed dreaming of the long delayed transition, which I felt was near realization, my mind wandered to a pearl-bedecked dress, pure and white, and before my mind's eyes there was materialized a beautiful corpse, robed in magnificent garments, which had been created for a bride, to whom every pearl, every thread had represented joyous anticipation of love's consummation. There was something fascinating about the picture, even in the contemplated arrangement of the hair, the manicuring of the nails, etc. So enamored did I become of robing my corpse in my wedding dress that I wanted to look into a mirror and see whether this enforced illness had left any traces on my face, as apprehensively I wondered whether the long agonizing weeks had written their story in lines on my face. Although I realized this was foolish, it was irresistible, and I felt compelled to see how I looked. I knew that I should be thinking of higher things and though I resisted the impulse as long as I could I was finally obliged to call the nurse and ask:

"Will you please bring me a mirror?—I want to see how I look."

"Very well," she assented smiling, as she turned away to comply with my request, and in a moment returned, handing me the glass, saying:

"Your illness has certainly dealt gently with your looks." I accepted her remark only as an encouragement and when she resumed her seat by the window I held the mirror in my hand hesitating to look—because I thought it possible that my appearance had changed. After pausing a little I looked. Uncertainty deepened into profound interest as I stared into the mirror. Not a line of my face nor the semblance of it did I see. Instead of the reflection of my face there was something alarmingly different—a garden in which the form of a man was kneeling with eyes upturned in reverential entreaty. It needed no one to tell me what this represented yet I was reluctant to admit it, and tried further to deceive myself by wondering what it meant refusing to accept what I *knew* it was and what everyone would recognize. I had, perforce, one might say, within the last few weeks accepted God, a Supreme Being, Infinite Intelligence—call it what you will—the Cause of which the earth life is the effect, but to accept the Christ seemed different, and yet there before my eyes was reflected in minute detail, as the orthodox would conceive it, the sublime agony in the Garden of Gethsemane.

It distressed me to behold this scene—I who at the same time was denying it and looking at it. I did not want to see it nor admit its existence. I had progressed so wonderfully near the World Beyond that encountering this vision on the threshold of it was like a bar to further progress. It was as if my greatest sin of omission had waited to halt me at the very gateway.

"No, not that, it cannot be," I told myself, as with a sigh of unrest I laid the glass face down on the bed and tried to convince myself that it was all a delusion, that my sight had become impaired by constantly seeing things that did not exist to the physical senses. And then, what had the story of this garden to do with me anyway? I knew there was an existence beyond this into which one passed through the process we call "death" but this did not compel the acceptance of all the theories of all the ages. I argued to myself that this Christ was only one of many Christs, recalling the beautiful story of Lord Buddha and the Saviours of other nations. Along these lines my thoughts wandered from the vision in the mirror into the realm of "stock" arguments against the Christ, which so fortified me mentally that I was quite confident that the vision had vanished and with this assurance I raised the mirror and again looked into it. I almost dropped it so great was the shock; it was nearer, much nearer and wonderfully magnified. I never looked upon anything that so affected me, especially so when I perceived that the figure in the garden was alive! As I looked fixedly at it the hands moved in supplication, the eyes tremblingly opened and shut in agony, and a great scintillating light came down above the head and played about the sorrowful face, while the lips quivered, the eye-lids stiffened and the eyes grew fixed in upward supplication.

I realized that this was the most wonderful scene that I had had the privilege of beholding. The hand of time had turned back to the Tragedy of Tragedies and bringing it up through the centuries, had placed it before my unbelieving eyes and I gazed at it in the very agony of its reality. Yes, there was the garden—the Garden of Gethsemane lay across my pathway—between me and the other world, and to go beyond it was to pass through it.

And the *living* scene held me as in a spell. I could not turn my eyes away; it held me in an awe that was painfully fascinating and a voice was whispering sorrowfully: "Gethsemane—Gethsemane," and soft voices took up the refrain farther and farther away until the very faintest echo came back "Gethsemane—Gethsemane." I then found myself staring in the mirror at the reflection of my own pale, disturbed face, to which I did not even notice for I realized the wonderful vision had gone. I laid the mirror down reverently, face up, and thought long and earnestly. All noises seemed sacriligious. I remember these words insinuated themselves into my thoughts:

"The same world still whether it smiles or scorns
That crowned Voltaire with roses, Christ with
thorns."

The vision seemed indelible. It was photographed on my mentality, and impressed upon my soul. I sought to fathom the mystery of it, a voice startled me saying:

"We are all Christs—the same divine spark is incorporated within all. He is the Son of God and all are the children of God."

How shocking this sounded for a moment but the "still, small voice" within, the divine spark, whispered and I *knew* it was true.

"He is the perfect man manifested; our Exemplar and teacher," continued the speaker. "When we evolve to where we are willing to die that others might live, we begin to recognize within ourselves the Christ Consciousness."

There was such a sense of being lifted up above and beyond the mundane, a sense of no longer belonging to the earth life, that when dinner was served it seemed an unnatural thing, a thing to be resented. How could one administer to the physical when the banquet halls of the soul were filled with feasts that money could not buy nor earth produce?

"And I feel the power uprising
    Like the power of an embryo God;
With a glorious wall it surrounds me
    And lifts me up from the sod."

In the stillness of the night these manifestations of the day came back persistently and re-enacted themselves, driving sleep away. I tried to shut them out by listening attentively to the heavy dashing of the sea against the rip-rap beyond the sea-wall and endeavored to fancy myself watching the spray as it splashed above the rocks and fell back in the foam of the sea but above all there was a garden scene that haunted my senses—the face of the "Man of Sorrows" shut out everything else. There was an invisible throng about me. I could hear them talking amongst themselves as in consultation and hear that compelling word "Gethsemane." Then magically a change came over everything and I stood in the garden where I had seen the Figure of Sorrow kneeling. I realized that standing there was a privilege that transcends conception. And even as this recognition was upon me I found that I was not alone; in some strange way this garden semed to embrace the whole world and the whole world was sorrowing deeply, and "the voice that was calmer than the silence," said:

"When I come again I will destroy this garden of sorrows."

Was it Christ telling me that he was coming again? I was asking myself in perplexity not unmixed with humility, as I looked pityingly upon the sorrow about me and then lifted my eyes beyond it to the other side, and, although the garden was dark but for the stars, beyond it there was a beacon light, illuminating the dark, silent waters beyond, to which the path through the garden led.

> "We may not know it but there lies
>   Somewhere under the evening skies
> A garden we all must see
>   Gethsemane, Gethsemane
> Each his own Gethsemane."

CHAPTER XVIII.

PASSING INTO THE BEYOND.

At breakfast the next day a voice said:
"Eat nothing; drink nothing," so the breakfast remained untasted, while I wondered at a command so strangely at variance with all mundane requirements. My obedience caused a veritable storm of protest from those interested in my physical welfare.

When my fiance came in the evening and remonstrated, I was strongly tempted to confess all but when this temptation was strongest, I remembered a motto hanging over his desk: "The Head That Is Loaded With Wisdom Does Not Leak At The Mouth," and refrained, realizing that my confession might be productive of more harm than good. I thus forced him to place his own construction on what appeared to be "obstinate foolishness" on my part.

The finest wines, delicacies and fruits were brought to me only to be carried away. I really did not want them, as I was neither hungry nor thirsty. In some splendidly beautiful way I was protected against the physical inconvenience and distress that otherwise would have attended so complete a fast.

It was then I felt most keenly the responsibility of living in two worlds—each exacting its obligations. To the requirements of the forces of earth, the invisible would not concede an inch and so between the two I was unhappily suspended—an intermundane creature, of neither world yet in both! I bore it all as patiently as I could, realizing that those interested in me were drawing as heavily on the Bank of Patience as I was and so tried to impress upon them my appreciation of the kindness of their intentions. They were toiling blindly in the darkness but I was moving toward the beacon light beyond the darkness, in unison with something they could not understand.

On the third day my Beloved came in the evening with a look of determination on his face, and after seating himself came characteristically straight to the point.

"I have never before asked favor of God, Man or Devil but I do ask you to be reasonable and to conform to the recognized requirements of life."

"Oh, Dear, please let's talk of something else," I pleaded, but he continued until he had said every word he intended and concluded by asking pointedly:

"Will you?"

"No," I replied, feeling that I had affixed my signature to my death warrant. He drew himself up with a sorrowful expression on his face and resentment in his eyes, and refrained from further comment on the subject.

I felt like screaming—to relieve the tenseness of the silence that had settled down upon us. When it seemed I could not endure it another moment, I said with pleading in my soul, whether it was in my voice or not.

"Talk to me, dear. Tell me something that has happened today."

"Nothing has happened," he answered looking straight ahead.

"Don't worry about me," I ventured, and added, "Can't you see that I am better?"

"Nonsense," he replied almost irritably, taking further refuge in the silence that so oppressed me.

I tried desperately to escape the influence of the oppressive silence but it was impossible. Then the tenseness began to give way—something seemed to snap—I was sinking—sinking—going out beyond the depression—beyond the range of argument.

Observing this, he turned to me calling:

"Fanny, Fanny," which I heard without the ability to respond. He took my cold hand, felt the pulse and turned to the nurse:

"Wine, please."

When she came with the wine he lifted my head and tried to pour it into my mouth but obedient to the force that dominated me, I turned my face away. The wine stained the white pillow without a drop going into my mouth.

This was too much. I saw his face almost convulsed with annoyance, which he restrained with a visible effort, as he set the glass down with precision, bade me an icicle-fringed good-night and left the house.

In semi-consciousness I listened to his retreating footsteps, all the time hoping that he would relent and come back but when I heard the gate click with more emphasis than usual I knew my wishing was in vain. That icy good-night seemed a living thing which tantalized and chilled me, making me feel like calling him back to explain to him, regardless of consequences, that my change of attitude was not a change of heart. This I wanted to tell him before the "cold hand" that lingered near touched me with the silence that would forbid the telling of what I felt he should know.

"Fanny," interrupted a voice from the invisible. I whispered "Hush—let me hold my love to my heart for the last time," and then—

"Why the last time?"

"I will soon be in another world."

"You have been taught that love does not suffer by the transition from world to world."

"So I have—so I have," I admitted more to myself than to the voice.

Then I heard the nurse creep quietly into bed as though she fancied me asleep. Soon I heard her sigh the sigh of weariness born of her unavailing efforts to tempt me from an allegiance she could not understand. That she soon slept was evidenced by a voice that said solemnly:

"She is asleep and cannot wake until she is freed."

I had felt no concern as to whether she slept or not, until this assertion made me wonder why her sleeping was required. As far as I was concerned the distressing happenings of the evening had "murdered sleep." Also it was *Tuesday* night, with the hand of fate pointing toward the end of uncertainty.

"Yes," I mentally admitted, "this *is* Tuesday night and there will be no more."

"Yes," echoed a voice, "but other Tuesday nights have found you equally assured." This had a dampening effect on my assurance but a rousing effect on my resentment. The thought of another week without the strength to endure it appalled me. Weak though I was I sat up in bed and looked out the window on the soft moonlit night, felt the gulf breezes on my already cold face and shivered. Oh, the wretchedness of it all! Weak and trembling I sat huddled up, with my arms about my knees, reviewing the events of the agonizing weeks that had passed, feeling anew resentment that this strange, strong strong force held me, making a plaything of my earnestness, causing me to wound and annoy those who loved me and whose love I cherished; holding me in the weak subjective condition of semi-illness, causing me to act as directed with all the earnestness of my soul only to be rewarded with deception and disappointment. I could not reconcile the events leading up to this night with the continuation of mundane existence. When I thought of the irony of the voice my very soul cried out in darkness:

"Why can't you be fair with me?"

Out of the stillness came a calm voice in rebuke:

"Can you not yet discern between truth and deception?"

"Forgive me," I whispered, contritely, "you know how weary I am." A flood of joy burst upon me and again the controlling Power held me passive.

Slowly I turned, adjusted the pillows, arranged my night clothing comfortably, shook my hair loose, pushed the covers away so they would not touch me and lay down, first in one position, then in another, in a vain effort to get comfortable.

As a soft hand pressed my forehead and caressed my hair a voice said tenderly:

"Remember the light beyond the darkness."

"Yes, the beacon light beyond Gethsemane," and I seemed to see it again nearer and more luminous than before.

"Peace be thine," came like a benediction, falling on the soft stillness; all weariness was gone and my soul was bathing itself in the floodtide of resignation as I whispered:

"I am thine, Oh, God, do with me as thou wilt," and closing my eyes in a resignation that was absolute, I realized that I was very cold with a coldness that held my hands and feet numb within its icy embrace. Then chilly waves touched my heart, slowing its pace. Little lights like miniature stars rose in the white cloud firmament that had formed in the room; the tiniest electric flashes, blue tinged, came and went; waves of soft variegated colors, undulating amid the whiteness, were spreading themselves into delicate tints; the air was perceptibly charged with electricity, the room vibrant with it and I was conscious of almost imperceptible shocks which gave an apprehensive feeling lest a real shock come. Then what seemed little detached electric lights, illuminated the whiteness in a most weird and fantastic manner during which time the shocks became quite distinct. Then into the electrified whiteness came forms and faces of ethereal, light-emitting, self-illuminating beings wrapped in ever-moving silvery vapor, that tinted everything with silver. White, transparent hands appeared only to hide themselves again within the mist, where faces, ever changing, were coming and going. Floating within the silvery mist were the faces of my parents. Lillian was there, too, with her happy, smiling face, near enough for me to touch. There came others I had known in the earth life smiling in welcome recognition. Dream faces came and went and voices chanted in harmony with the "choir invisible" while I felt a conscious at-one-ness with the manifestations which surrounded me.

Then slowly there came down an unconfined electric-laden lightness, which spread over me, touching me at first cautiously and lightly with an undulating movement, which caused perceptible shocks. It would touch me and draw away when the shocks became too pronounced, only to return and repeat the process again and again until finally the shocks were no longer perceptible and I had the sensation of being a part of them, of being electrified, as it were. Then with a vibrating, quivering movement it spread itself over my body, enveloping me entirely, holding me within itself, as it settled down with a suggestion of permanency. It was with considerable wonder I tried to analyze this strange scintillating, vital, *living* essence. It was a live thing without any sign of life, I could see it without seeing it, feel it without feeling it, as it held me in its magnetized embrace; it gave the impression of the very essence of power, occupying unlimited space, inter-penetrating all things indefinable yet holding all things subject to its law. It was a kind of white fire but without the faintest suggestion of fire as we know it.

"Can this wonderful—this beautiful thing be death?"

"It is birth—there is no death," voices chanted back and in unison with these musical voices, I joined in "It is birth—there is no death," which lifted my soul higher and higher in wonderful realization.

I knew it was what we term "death"—the separation of the soul and body, that which we look upon as something horrible, a thing to be avoided at all costs and as long as possible; yet I held it to me as the most wonderful and beautiful experience that life had ever given me.

I knew I was "going out"—drifting out over the borderland, through the Channel of Death unto the Sea of Life Everlasting, which is supposed to give up its mysteries only to those who sail upon its waters.

I could feel my blood turning cold—could feel the

physical body growing heavy and still. There was not even a suggestion of pain. Then I was conscious of something moving, something struggling within and knew it was the "shadow" body struggling for release—the soul freeing itself from its prison of flesh.

Little lapses of consciousness came and went as the "Shadow" body adjusted and readjusted its sails and helm in conformity with the beacon light ahead, as the shore it was leaving became dimmer and dimmer. Suddenly it stopped upon the "still waters" of the channel and as seabird to its mate, it called to a loved one who remained on the darkening shore, "good-bye, my love." While lingering in regret that the voice could not span the distance between them, the beloved face seemed to come and mingle with the dream faces within the silvery mist, just as though it were one of them instead of a human being in the earth life. Again the magic word "good-bye" was whispered and the departing soul then renewed its struggles against the tides of the receding shore, with eyes fixed on the beacon light beyond the dark channel.

Night began "casting shadows before," hiding the dream faces, obscuring the lights, hushing the music. Then suddenly came an impact in the right side, defined but painless, causing a perceptible start.

The night was come—it was dark, so dark—I was alone on the mystic sea of the silence.

"Welcome to Death,
If thou, oh, Death, a being art, draw near
 And let me clasp thee; for I hold thee dear.
I shall extract eternal life from thee;
 Thou cans't but snatch this worn out dress from
  me."

CHAPTER XIX.

OVER THE BORDERLAND.

It was very dark and I was wondering where the dream faces had gone—where the lights were—in fact, what had happened.

In my perplexity I began casting vaguely about but there was nothing to touch. It was all space, just empty space—and the bed, where was it? It dawned upon me that I was suspended somewhere, somehow; and from that base I began trying to make observations. All about and above me I could see nothing, but fancy my astonishment if you can, when looking down, I saw my body resting peacefully on the bed, representing what is commonly called a "dead person." I could not move my eyes from it; it fascinated me as it lay in the cold whiteness, robed in a gown of lavendar silk, with dainty laces and ruffles. The neck and arms were bare, as were the feet; the hair lay loose and disheveled, with little brown curls on the white forehead. The deep blue "windows of the soul," the eyes, were at half mast; the soul being absent the light was gone; the lips, slightly parted wore just a suggestion of a smile; the left hand rested lightly on the breast—the engagement ring scintillating as brightly as ever; the right, which no doubt had been lifted unconsciously at the shock of impact, had fallen a little apart from the body and lay, palm upturned. How peaceful it looked! Thus every detail of the clay image fastened itself upon my consideration as I viewed it dispassionately, realizing that it was a cast-off garment for which I had no further use. However, I felt a protective kindliness toward it; it had been a faithful servant, executing my every wish and whim and now that I had passed beyond the range of its services, it pleased my fancy to robe it in the white, pearl-bedecked dress, the wearing of which, had meant so much to me in quite a different way.

A disturbing thought obtruded itself—how differently *he* would look upon that which I was contemplating with complacency! This changed the focus of my interest and I turned my eyes away in the darkness, with the desire heavy upon me to go to him and let him know that I still lived—that it was "not all of life to live nor all of death to die;" that the passage across the dark channel intensifies rather than abates love. As though responding to my thought I felt myself moving, or being propelled by a vibratory sensation. It seemed to last but a moment. Then I stopped and, instinctively looking down, I saw sleeping beneath me the object of my solicitude. As I looked upon him I saw the shadow body more distinctly than the physical. Viewed from the other side of life, the "shadow" body seemed the original and the physical the duplicate, the soul the real, the body the unreal. Within and interpenetrating all was a light, which I had not before perceived as being a part of the spiritual anatomy. This light penetrated from *within,* both the shadow and physical bodies, maintaining through and about the body an aura or illumination which enveloped it; clothing it, as it were, in a magnetized illumination. How wonderful this three-in-one life-manifestation seemed, especially when we generally recognize only the one—the physical!

Someway, how different he seemed! It was like a mental vivisection. Yet the difference of viewpoint was the only difference, I concluded, as I moved a little nearer and called low so that I might not startle him from his slumber.

"Dearest, I am here," I said mentally, in the very same way that I had conversed with the invisibles before my transition, but he slept on. His soul which was *not* sleeping responded joyously and tried to help me pass the perception of my presence into his physical consciousness. He moaned and turned restlessly in his sleep, as I called to him again and again. Then in a disturbed way, he moved and called out:

"Fanny, Fanny," as wide awake he sat up in bed, and said:

"Such dreams—I deamed she was dead." So he had really heard without recognizing it.

Now that he was awake I came yet a little nearer, confident that he would see and hear me, for I stood very near him and called softly: "I am here, dear," but he only seemed more restless and sighed more deeply. Then with nervous impatience he turned on the light, reached for his glasses and a magazine which were on the stand beside his bed, muttering:

"Such a night—no rest—no sleep." He was thinking sorrowfully of the possibility of my death as he adjusted his glasses, turned one of the pillows on end to make his head higher, and settled down to read, despite the fact that I stood near, calling to him, charging the very atmosphere with sentiment and eagerness. In a hurt way I drew back and suddenly, as though for the first time, the full realization came upon me, and in an awed way, I whispered to myself:

"I am *dead*, that is why he cannot hear and see me," and yet I felt more *alive* than I had ever felt. I was the same person in every way. There was something pitiably painful about being so near one beloved, seeing him plainly and hearing him distinctly, even knowing that he was thinking of me, and yet having him utterly ignore my presence, and above all knowing that he would never recognize me again —never hear my voice no matter how ardently I called, while I was the same in every way minus the physical body.

Then I fell to wondering why he could not hear or see me and perceived that the vibratory environment in which I was held did not harmonize with that which encompassed him, yet touched so intimately that even as I watched, I hoped for a harmonious blending of these vibratory waves, which gave the impression of "cross currents" in the sea. Mine was the vibration of perpetual motion—his more like a "dead sea" into which these vibratory currents ebbed and flowed, and it seemed such an easy matter to move out of the "deadness" into the "ebb and flow" that I waited and watched a long time before I realized that he would make *no* effort to do so. With this realization full upon me, I looked at him calmly, without expecting him to see or to hear, acknowledging that my mission had failed and wishing that I could explain it all to him. Looking down into his troubled face, I moved a little nearer and called to him again without expecting any response:

"Au revoir, my love—until we meet again." Then with a strange soul sadness I turned away and would have moved on when I perceived the vibratory force was holding me, steadily restraining any further movement. I began to wonder and to chide myself for mundane interests beyond which I realized I had passed. Persistently the force held me, as though inviting me to further consideration of earth interests, but I had none. My material possessions were disposed of as I desired; there was no life-work I was leaving incomplete; I had no children, no one depending on me; nothing held me to the earth. My desire had been to go beyond it and now that I had done so, I was well pleased and wanted to go on to the joys I felt awaited me beyond the influence of the earth. Yet the force held me, try as I would to pass beyond it, until, instead of struggling against it, I tried to understand it—to wrest from it its reason for thus detaining me, feeling that there must be some reason for such marked persistence. Almost instantly the lesson sank into my consciousness and I realized that the long arm of mundane interests can reach into the Beyond and hold its victims within the shadow of earth—pitting its magnetism against the promise of higher things.

Then I was moving easily in an undulating way, within the propelling vibration and when I stopped darkness enveloped me—not a sight nor a sound—just oppressive heavy darkness, with the sensation of being alone in eternity weighing heavily upon me, as I waited in awesome uncertainty.

At first this darkness was appalling, the silence oppressive; but I was not long in perceiving that this, too, had its part to play in the great scheme of things, as I could feel a wonderful, new strength manifesting within me. My sight grew, until it overcame the darkness and I perceived that I was not alone nor was it dark—that the darkness had been within me and could be eliminated only from within. There were loved ones and many others welcoming me and rejoicing that I was with them. Meon also was there at which I rejoiced exceedingly, feeling vaguely that where he was there could be no uncertainty. How carefree and light I felt!

Again came that indescribable sensation of being held within that electric-laden, *living* light that had come upon and enveloped me, just before my transition. It now gave the impression of a kind of invisible, living elevator. It was still holding me within itself with all of its electrified, weird, vibratory power and I wondered that it was no longer a *light*. As I wondered, it emitted a faint blue-tinged illumination, giving the impression that it was a light, only as it elected, or occasion required.

As I quivered within the strangeness of it all, Meon fastened his dark, luminous eyes upon me, and asked solemnly:

"And having come, whither goest thou?" Rather a disturbing question one must admit when I was trying to adjust myself to the condition of having *come!* And now I was to *go?* I remember feeling that if he did not know any more about it than I did, we were in a more deplorable plight than the "Babes in the Woods." As I deliberated, not altogether pleased at assuming such a colossal responsibility, Meon, knowing my thoughts, interrupted:

"Weaver of thy Freedom, Choose." Again that phrase!—it had followed me even into eternity which fact I half resented but since I was confronted with choosing my destiny, in a world of which I knew nothing, and since hope had painted beautiful and alluring pictures of a soul's ideal; feeling that the time had come for ideals to become real, I cried out in exultation:

"To the very highest Heaven."

"That is well," he made answer evenly, as the electrified vibrations began manifesting and he stood in a listening attitude which I simulated. In a moment I distinctly heard the word "Come" and with a soft, bluish light playing about and enveloping us, we floated out on the undulating waves of space.

CHAPTER XX.

THE RED DARKNESS.

As we floated I noted that the vibratory waves by which we were propelled were not unlike those which had propelled my hand to write independently of my direction and realized that the same power was, in like manner, propelling my body through space.

And so we went on until I could see fringing the darkness red light or rather a red darkness, which held my attention until we came within it when the sensation of being among many excluded all other considerations. I was listening, trying to hear what they were saying but the vibrations were evidently not in harmony, so I could not hear distinctly, and after a long time of vain effort I turned to Meon, and asked:

"What place is this?"

"Let Perception be your teacher," he replied curtly.

"Tell me, please," I persisted, with increasing interest.

"Ask no questions—that which is for you to know will be given without asking."

Thus rebuked I took refuge in silence. Then—surely I was mistaken—it was only fancy, a horrible fancy, those agonizing groans and cries! But slowly a terrible knowledge sifted into my consciousness—I knew what a burdensome thing memory could be and listening carefully I learned many other things from the environment about me.

"Are we near the earth?" I asked, feeling convinced that we were.

"Yes, within its magnetism or spiritual gravitation."

"Why are these beings detained here?"

"They are not detained. Some desire it while others are not yet strong enough to progress beyond it."

"Why?"

"Earth's interests hold them."

I would have questioned further but remembered what Meon had said and restrained myself, feeling grateful for the information that he had given and turning again to Perception, as my teacher.

As I listened discriminatingly I heard cries of the "might have been;" of lives wasted in the making; of derelicts tossed by the waves of circumstances; of those who had failed creatures depending on them; cries of vengeance unexecuted; of vengeance executed; of crimes unpardonable and unpardoned; earth ties of weakness; a consuming love of earth and the pleasures thereof; of those who wanted to go back if only for an hour to right wrongs they had fastened upon some earth being; of those who were afraid to go on and wanted to come back. Horrible to listen to and pitiful to contemplate. There was no bar to their going on but they did not want to; some did not know they could. It was the earth that attracted them—the earth that held them—they felt they could not give up the earth life. So intimately was the connection between this place and the earth that I could hear living, loving human beings of earth, because of these invisible influences, crying out in their anguish in a hopeless way; could hear them saying,

"Earth is Hell—Earth is Hell," as they suffered on without knowing the cause.

In this dark earth-magnetized region disembodied spirits lived the mundane existence much as the psychic lives the spiritual while yet in the mundane— one is progression, the other retrogression. Disembodied spirits living the mundane life do so at the expense of human beings in the earth life, while the mundane person living the spiritual life is obeying the law of evolution and progression.

It is this condition which requires discrimination on the part of the investigator.

I heard the voices, felt the touches of these derelicts, outcasts and fallen creatures of the Spirit World and my heart cried out in pity for them as I wondered if this condition was permanent or by what process this spiritual blindness was treated. As I wondered my perception quickened, enlarging my spiritual vision and I saw descending into the redness spirits of love and mercy illuminating the way as they came down, calling, calling as they came and while all of the submerged had not yet acquired spiritual hearing some had and I could hear an occasional answering voice struggling up from the vortex, "I am coming," and I knew that some were passing beyond it. Also I was given to know what a powerful influence earth beings could exert in sending them on their journey instead of permitting them to exercise influence and propensities at their expense. Then and there I wanted to tell the suffering, toiling creatures of earth that they were not compelled to submit to such influences; that no matter how strong the influence of evil is, the God principle incorporated within every human being is stronger, making us superior to all other forces. If we could only recognize this within *ourselves*—this divine essence that makes us *one* with the source of all life, power and infinitude we could not only free our souls from uncertainty, our bodies from disease, plague, madness, murders and unhappiness but could help these souls of darkness to turn toward the light into the vibratory waves of progression and realize that

"Knowledge is the wings wherewith
We fly to Heaven."

The one thing I would like to impress upon every one is *there is no soul irretrievably lost,* no matter how many aeons it may remain in darkness (and long and many are the journeys some make before the light of truth floods their consciousness).

As I was vibrating about trying to learn all I could of the place I became aware that souls were passing on, going beyond this Red Darkness, and I in turn was filled with a desire to pass beyond it. Then came a chilling fear—horror of horrors—was *this* my destination?

Meon relieved my suspense promptly:

"Did not the Christ descend into this place before his ascension?"

The word "Hell" intruded itself upon my consciousness although there was nothing suggestive of the orthodox Hell of fire and brimstone. It was red but certainly not fire, nor did it have any of the attributes of fire. I could not shake off the conviction that it was Hell none the less—made up of souls who, while on earth, had been so entirely dominated by the flesh, that the separation from that domination, caused them in their very soul weakness to look back upon the physical as a thing superior to themselves.

Feeling assured that I was not to remain in this environment, I went boldly further into the darkness, as if to wrest every secret from it, but I had not gone far when a voice from the very depths arrested me and I fell back listening and a voice unlike any I had yet heard was saying:

"Earth's sins gave this place existence; earth's magnetism maintains it."

Somehow I did not care to penetrate any further and grew retrospective. "Descended into Hell," kept recurring to me until it became my theme of thought. I remembered (a memory not altogether pleasant just then) that that had been one of my stock and, according to my version, most effective arguments against the existence of the Christ. I recalled the number of Gods or Christs that according to Theological History (and Mythological) had "descended into Hell and risen again the third day." There were Krishna, the Hindoo God; Zoroaster, the Persian God; Osiris, Egyptian God; Baldur, Scandinavian God; Quetzalcoatle, Mexican God; as well as the virgin-born saviors Horus, Adonis, Bacchus, Hercules and Mercury, the Word and Messenger of God. Many Christs in many different religions. There was the beautiful story of Lord Buddha. Meon interrupted gently:

"To all nations has been given their ideal man—their teacher, as an example of man's possibilities. One for the whole world will now suffice but when these ideals came nations knew less of each other than they did of God."

What a difference one's viewpoint can make of the same circumstances! In the Christ argument that which had been the ultimate in the negative now occupied the same position in the affirmative.

As I pondered over these things I felt myself again within the vibratory propelling force and heard the word, "Come."

I regret a sense of duty compels me to incorporate within a book the undesirable condition just described. I would choose, were the choice mine, to embody only that which is beautiful and uplifting. Personally, I have always opposed the theory of evil, believing with Shakespeare, "Nothing is evil but thinking makes it so," but in our daily lives when we face *facts* instead of theories we know that evil (call it what you will—that which is disagreeable to us) exists, regardless of what our theories may or may not be. We admit that evil has no power except what *we* give it; and yet we *know* that every day we cope with something that tries to tear us away from our ideals and standards of life, making us realize that "The post of honor is a private station," while we go on living our double lives—the lives we *intend* to live and the lives we *really* live.

CHAPTER XXI.

"THE POWER HOUSE OF EXISTENCE."

There were many questions I would have asked Meon as we went along but felt instinctively that it would be useless, as he had advised, "Let perception be your teacher," therefore I was acting in accordance in so far as I could.

All about me the air was charged with moving beings, going ever onward, some going swiftly, while others plodded along as though their burdens had not been sufficiently lightened for the requirements of the journey.

While noting all this I discovered that I could see back of me, to the right or to the left as easily as I could in front, as though my body saw as well as my eyes. This strange new faculty of observation gradually increased my scope of vision.

Far out beyond the red-fringed darkness I could see light, in which rainbows seemed to play, pale as the dawn, of a gray-weird loveliness, coming and going as though flirting with the darkness, for to embrace it would be to destroy. For delicate beauty it seemed I had never seen anything more fascinating or alluring than this kiss of the dawn and the darkness in the Soul world—it was like life kissing death goodbye.

With this mystical and lovely dawn of another world upon me, I lost in the witchery of it, we landed suddenly on what had every appearance of being an earth. There were houses, flowers, trees; everything was so life-like it amazed me. I almost fancied I had returned to earth. The light was dim as of the dawn and a cool peaceful gentleness permeated everything, as the inhabitants moved about in a free, easy and unrestrained way. They conversed with me as though they considered me a spirit of the higher world, asking me questions of the "life to come," as we might of one who comes from the realms beyond the earth. They were full of faith, love and certainty as to an "after life" and seemed spiritually far in advance of the earth, yet they were perfectly familiar with earth-life and its conditions, evidently having lived on earth, nor were they entirely free from the magnetism of earth interests, as I saw some going earthward, as though drawn by something of paramount importance. They would dive, as it were, quickly and easily, into the Red Darkness and gradually become one with its redness.

While there seemed no doubt that these people once inhabited the earth, I saw no one I had ever known in this life. They had possibly progressed there out of the darkness and would go back to help those less fortunate into the higher condition which they had attained.

As I wondered at it all, the dimness of the soft, silvery light and other things which I did not understand, a voice came:

"To eyes grown accustomed to the darkness this light is brilliant."

"It is beautiful—very beautiful" I said, as the admitted mercy of its softness, added to its loveliness, held me in mystic dreaminess until the command "come" called me beyond its environment and I went wondering—and I am still wondering.

For my own convenience I called this place of existence the "Dawn World," for so it seemed, as it was there the light began to neutralize the darkness for those whose nights had been very long and whose dreams had been bad.

As we vibrated onward in the ever increasing light passing silent shadow cities under the radiance of great orbs, we seemed to be riding on the very air in company with countless thousands, everything vibrating onward in perpetual motion.

So enchanting was this riding on vibratory waves of space (not entirely unlike those of the sea) in a gentle undulatory way, that I felt like going on forever, and forever, never tiring, never stopping but after abandoning myself to the witchery of it for some time, I perceived the vibrations changing, merging into a quivering sensation, even more exquisite, and then, as if a part of it, my feet came upon something different, something firm and reliable, as one

"Treads upon the void and finds
The rock beneath."

Wonderful was the sight that met my enraptured gaze! A city of light and of whiteness, boundless in expanse. I walked in this place very much as I had on earth, for it seemed I had reached the limit of my ability to float in space, it seemed that I was heavier than my surroundings in some way. Everywhere were the most exalted souls I had yet seen. Some came forward and greeted us, addressing Meon as though he were one of them, and then, together, we entered into a building immeasurable in space and height, the veritable soul of architectural magnificence. The material had the transparency of glass of a variegated whiteness, into which colors, harmonizing in the most delicate way, were coming and going, ever changing. Electricity seemed to be the power which held it all together, as the electric blue would merge into violet and play incessantly, in a serpentine way, into which almost imperceptible yellowish streams seemed to flow. It was self-illuminated. This is not a very accurate description but really I am not master of the words that it requires, so we will just have to let it go at that, with the hope that some day, when we are more familiar with such matters, some enterprising person will compile a dictionary for the convenience of those who will write describing our future homes.

The floor was even more transparent, with less color, and vibrated as the beating of a pulse. Treading upon it sent strange thrills through my entire body, as though harmonizing the body with its magnetism. At first this was not altogether a pleasant sensation but after getting into harmony with it all mysteries seemed dissolved; the very atmosphere exuded knowledge, free and flowing for the mentality to feed upon as there is only the mentality to sustain; just as in the earth life, air is free and flowing to give breath to the physical body.

It seemed that all the wisdom of all the ages was mine as I stood there. Life and death gave up their mysteries, and I no longer wondered but observed as one who understood. The machinery of earth existence was operated and regulated by and through the power of this plane. It was actually in contact with the earth. No happening on earth escaped the observation of the great spirits who seemed to have nothing else to do but watch over the beings of earth, to teach them, to lift them up, to protect and help them up through the darkness; watch over reincarnations, create teachers and place them where they were most needed. With these teachers they were in direct communication at all times and knew exactly what was going on through some form of wireless telegraphy or telephony, perhaps, but they communicated as though there were no distance. They seemed to draw the highly evolved souls of earth up to them mentally, and these cooperated consciously, responding unerringly. It was marvelous to watch the process or rather processes, as there were many phases of this supervision. They were coming and going all the time. I saw many go out and disappear into the depths, all rejoicing in their work, the uplifting of humanity. The souls were countless, the space immeasurable, yet there was no confusion—it was system idealized, each recognizing his mission and doing it. Truly it was the Christ principle manifested, for they were laboring for others, not themselves.

For my own convenience I designated this place, "The Power House of Existence" and even now I cannot think of anything more appropriate, so we will just let it go at that.

Once again I was conscious of being held within that great self-illuminating electrified current that had made itself manifest all along the way. Now, it not only held me but interpenetrated, holding within itself even this great "power house" which had so impressed me with its importance that it seemed there could be nothing greater. I looked with a new interest upon the living fluid within it, saw it spreading itself out before me, going out into the violet-gold space, illuminating as it went, lighting up the darkness, even the red darkness, until I could see the far away earth, small in the distance; and could see souls all along the way held within its magnetized embrace, could see it touch the earth in the same careful, vibratory way that it had touched my body, an atom of earth. And again I asked myself—what is this invisible, silent ghost-like power that seems to be the living essence in everything? Suddenly it either greatly magnified the earth or gave me telescopic vision, for I could see the earth plainly, could feel it vibrate and tremble in unison with the "Power House" in which I stood, and up through this living current I could hear the voices of its people. Over all was a sense of a *living* connection between this place and the earth, as the darkness slowly obscured the earth and my vision passed out of harmonious vibrations with the electrified essence. While my senses lost sight of its presence there was something within me that made me know that there was no such thing as passing beyond its influence, as it interpenetrated all things. I still looked down into the blue-gold space without seeing, but the earth had taken on a new interest for me. Those about me had spoken of it as the most important phase of existence and I wondered how I could have been so blindly indifferent while the privilege of its existence was upon me. That hitherto obscure phrase, "The Brotherhood of Man," (which theory I had often laughed to scorn) prodded me with its importance. There had been something glorious in the recognition and admission of my *oneness* with God, Infinitude; but now I knew that I must also recognize and admit, in the same way, my oneness with *mankind* for "God has made of one blood all nations of men." And even yet further was the acknowledgment of my oneness with all *living* things, animate and inanimate; for the inanimate evolutes into the animate, the animate into animals, animals into man and man into God; "The race of men and God is one." Man is as God and exercises the God perogative to that which is in the scale below him and dependent on him; recognition of and action in accordance with this responsibility would greatly facilitate the problem of existence. Nor is there any sex in soul—the same soul sometimes functions as a male—sometimes as a female in the cycles of reincarnation. Referring to reincarnation, every step I took fastened its reality more firmly on me. It is, to me, the only explanation of the inequalities of life as I saw them all along the way. Reincarnation is the key to evolution—evolution the key to existence in an individualized way.

A great new love was in my heart for the people and the living things of earth. I sorrowed deeply because of their blindness, which caused most of their unhappiness and desired to go back and tell them what I had seen and what I knew that it might alleviate conditions in even the smallest way. A voice interrupted as I meditated:

"The first flush of the sunrise is even now upon the earth."

This, however, did not deter me in my desire to go back. In fact, I gave very little thought as to the meaning of the sentence. The desire to go back was growing, becoming more and more intense until it seemed as I stood looking far down into the fathomless space, that I could hear the earth calling me—

calling me, strange fantasy! With this desire full upon me, I turned to Meon and said:

"Meon, I want to go back."

He made no answer but looked at me with a strange triumph in his eyes, saying:

"Come."

Forthwith we moved from the earth's registration center and went higher up within the same environment where the influence of the earth was not felt so intimately. A great soul came forward as I went in and asked just as though I had told him:

"And you would return to earth?"

"Yes; if by so doing I could accomplish good."

"Suppose you could not, would you try regardless of what it might mean to you?"

"I am not considering myself—I want others to know what I know; it would make life so splendidly different."

"Suppose they would not believe you?"

"I would like to give them the opportunity, whether they would or not."

"Did the welfare of the people always interest you?"

"No."

"What has caused this change of sentiment?"

"Your splendid example and the process by which I have been shown earth's necessity."

"Would you suffer torture that another might pass into freedom?"

"I feel that I would endure *anything* that would uplift humanity."

"All experience that sensation when it is too late," said the voice sorrowfully and I was left alone with my new born desire, which did not change but rather intensified, despite the discouraging remark that had concluded the interview. I felt almost rebellious, as though I would go back anyway regardless of all opposition or opinions to the contrary and tell what I knew regardless as to whether people believed it or not.

Alone, removed from the direct influence of the earth and the great spirits, I viewed the matter dispassionately from all points, and the more I thought of it the more enamored I became of the project and the more determined in its execution, at the same time fully realizing that there were other forces to be taken into consideration in a co-operative sense, for in the great scheme of things there is no independence;

"All are parts of one stupendous whole
Whose body nature is and God the soul."

Alone in that ether-electricity, *one* with the very soul of things, in the intensity of my desire to return to earth with a message of knowledge and love, I lifted my eyes and there before me was a familiar face—the one I had seen in the garden before leaving the earth place; the agony was gone out of the face and it was radiant with love and promise, at the sight of which my soul rose up in pleading and I cried out:

"Let it be so—let it be so," and again I was alone with bowed head, the intensity of the desire burning within me, feeling that it was not in vain; for something deep down within me was saying: "Christ, too, is going back."

CHAPTER XXII.

PANORAMA OF LIFE AS LIVED ON EARTH.

When I again raised my eyes, vibrating directly before me was a little light, so tiny that, at first, I ignored it, but its persistence and magnetic attraction compelled my attention, which I gave rather reluctantly at first, then eagerly as it began shaping itself into something. As it vibrated it would disappear downward only to reappear larger and brighter than before. What was the meaning of it?

Then it appeared several times, illuminating different human faces, alternating male and female. It was not unlike a moving picture. Now it seemed to stand still before me larger and brighter than ever and more compelling in its attractiveness. As it started vibrating, a small, white, diaphanous, globe-like formation appeared around it and grew with it. In the growing it was no longer a tiny light within a tiny globe; it was a pretty, delicate baby face that smiled innocently into mine. So tiny and helpless it was that it appealed to me. Then I was given to know that this bit of humanity represented myself as I had come into this cycle of earth existence. As I gazed upon it, it merged into a doll-faced curly-haired, blue-eyed girl, incorporated within which I could still see the little light, bright and radiating, within the globe of white, which was within a "shadow" body, that in turn, interpenetrated and grew with the physical.

School days came and I heard people saying "she is the brightest girl in school." Still she grew as the little light within glowed in harmony with the great light that interpenetrates all things.

At this stage of the metamorphosic process I realized that it was truly *myself,* as I recognized the incidents portrayed as pages from the book of my schooldays, just as my memory retained them. Yet, I was looking upon this creature dispassionately, just as though it were someone else and in describing it I shall do so as if it were. It is so much easier to write in the third person, to say nothing of sparing the reader a whole life history of *I's.*

We will go back and take up this frail little creature as she revels in music, the one grand passion before which all things else seem as nothing. It holds her in bondage to itself, as she grows in the joy and mastery of it. How the little, white fingers, too small to span an octave, subconsciously caught fragments from the "choir invisible" and imprisoned them on the piano!

At college the last practice period in the evening was in what was termed the "haunted music room," where most of the girls dared not go after nightfall, so demoralizing was the story of the haunt but there was something about the mystery of it that appealed to this girl and made her prefer it to any of the other rooms, although the piano was the most ill-toned as well as ill-tuned in school. And now I even saw the ghost of the old music room standing beside her as she played—after all there *was* a ghost, regardless of the fact that she had laughed to scorn the idea. How strange it seemed to actually see it now after all these years!

With the coming of young womanhood I saw falling upon her a mantle which was labeled "SELF

RESPONSIBILITY." It came upon her suddenly, covering her from head to feet, yet she was as unconscious of its coming as she was of its potentiality and went on just as though it had not come. As it spread itself upon her there appeared before her three roads; one was labeled "GOOD" one "EVIL" and the other, the center, was unlabeled. There were thousands treading the center road where there were hundreds on the others. There were many more upon the road of "Good" than upon that of "Evil." These roads were guarded by invisible creatures, according to the indicated propensities of each, who were always calling to those who traveled in the center, in an endeavor to influence them to more determined tendencies. Ever and anon there were paths leading from the center to the outer roads and from one outer road to the other, showing how easily one can change ones course at will.

I saw the girl's feet upon the unmarked road, saw her disappear in the onward moving rush and heard the voices calling, calling to those who heeded and those who heeded not.

When she came before me again there were two great shadows—twin shadows, as it were, hovering over her. One was labeled "Ambition," the other "Selfishness," and under cover of these shadows I saw her dreaming, dreaming, ever dreaming; the mirage was a great singer; the compensation, the homage of the world. I saw her holding to her heart in enchanted fancy, as the only thing worth while, the emptiest of all life's coveted cups—Fame.

With these terrible, dark shadows hovering over her,—touching her, her eyes glowed, her heart beat wildly, as she played on and on—sang on and on, ever dreaming of that magical "some day" on which she would sing as only dream singers can!

When night came, instead of lifting her fair, girlish face that the light within might consciously receive the illuminating influence of the greater light, she crept into bed, forgetful of all things except the object of her dreaming and there was no one to remind her that "by ambition fell the angels."

Then slowly, as by absorption, the twin shadows crept within the white globe, staining it and dimming the light within, unconscious of which she happily dreamed on. That "globe" effect was so peculiar that it is hard to describe so it can be understood, but I'll do my best. At first it was somewhat like an ordinary globe around any light, only it was nebulous; but as the bodies (the spiritual and physical) began manifesting and growing, it took on rather an oblong shape, interpenetrating and extending out beyond the bodies several feet, giving the suggestion of being the illumination from the little light that still remained within the bodies, the life spark, as it were. Colors came and went within it but they were very unlike these dark red-hued shadows that insinuated themselves into the whiteness about the head and spilled downward. Spirits of love and mercy focused their influence upon her, looking with sadness upon the shadows which the sport period of "self responsibility" had fastened upon her. Spirits of another kind came and smilingly whispered their approbation and encouragement, as her "Spanish Castles" grew to mighty proportions.

At last school days were over and I saw a proud, self-centered woman at a health resort, laughing, dancing and singing, with a heart as light and carefree as that of a bird. The world was good to her. She sang on, dreamed on, holding to her heart a passionate prayer to the Gods of destiny.

In the next scene she was sitting with a magazine on her lap, idly turning the pages, her thoughts far away, tangled in the meshes of illusion, delirious with its soft caresses. Great souls of the Invisible world stood beside her consulting as to her welfare, looking sadly upon the shadow stained globe but noting with satisfaction the pure whiteness where the shadows were not. Other spirits nearby were listening curiously, some joyously, some sadly, all realizing the seriousness of the consultation except the one most vitally concerned.

After some discussion and earnest deliberation one of the great souls said, with finality:

"Take away the *cause* of the shadows—it is the only way."

Then the great spirits went away sorrowfully, leaving her at least one more day of joy in her castle on the sands, before the tide would come and wash it away.

Something of what had transpired sifted into her consciousness, as she became restless and depressed —"blue" without knowing why. Apprehensive forebodings, indefinable but insistent, obtruded themselves upon her so forcibly that she laid the magazine down, arose, shook it all off and went singing to her room, where she arrayed herself in her most beautiful and becoming gown and went to a rehearsal of a society amateur theatrical to sing her "swan song," the encores of which she held to her heart as an advance consignment of the world's homage.

After the dancing began, a theatrical man made

the world her very own by saying:

"The world will hear of your singing some day—I feel that I have made a *find.*"

"Thank you," I heard her say, smiling serenely, regardless of the riotous triumph within.

"Would you accept an engagement?"

She looked at him in surprise and shrank away. Her dream had not progressed to that materialistic stage—the magical "Someday" was hid somewhere behind an alluring veil, far away in the dim future, with many days to dwell in dreamland before its coming. Accordingly she made answer almost indifferently:

"Not just yet—some day—perhaps."

"Mistake—you are making a mistake—there is no practice like stage practice for a stage career," he hastily admonished.

"Perhaps," I heard her say, as she gave him her permanent address before whirling away in a waltz, delirious with triumph. She danced until the hours were small and went home and sat for a long time dreaming the old dreams in a higher key and then slept as only the carefree can.

How vividly I recalled every incident as I saw it re-enacted in this ethereal realm far away from the earth, but it was hard to recognize this passionate, fame-mad creature as myself. It had been so long since I had enjoyed such rapturous madness that it seemed to have been in some former incarnation instead of only a few short years before.

All the details of this *living* picture I shall not inflict upon the reader but in this review of my earth life even the most trivial incident was not omitted. Its faithfulness to detail was perfectly marvelous.

Nothing was hidden, nothing slurred over. It was *all* there. I was standing face to face with my earth life just as I had lived it, awaiting its condemnation or justification. In writing this, however, I am confining myself to the most important incidents or main thread, which is sufficient to show the interest and influence of the invisible world on our earth lives individually, showing that while they respect the law of self-responsibility they interfere when it is used or abused to the detriment of the soul and operate or cooperate according to the law of soul progression. It is the exercise of this prerogative that sometimes changes the most joyous life into a living death from a mundane viewpoint, but fortunately the mundane is not the only viewpoint. If one cannot or will not grow strong spiritually and be happy at the same time, happiness is removed, that the soul may have its exercise on the dumb bells of misery and thereby grow strong, as spiritual strength is the only thing worth while that we can take with us when we cross over the Borderland.

There was a marked interval between the showing of the happy, triumphant girl and the sick woman who lay on a bed of agony the next morning. She was ill, very ill, with a cold, or hoarseness that grew so alarmingly worse that a physician came and diagnosed "Laryngitis." Without realizing the seriousness of it she wondered how she had "caught such a cold," and felt it would be entirely dissipated within a few days.

But when another day gave place to another and yet another she knew different; she realized that she was very ill—down in the "valley of the shadow."

Breathing became so difficult that every effort, artificial and otherwise, was made to facilitate it.

I could see the "shadow" body within struggling to free itself, to pass beyond its bondage which it seemed to realize would thereafter be a bondage indeed—a veritable prison house of expiation. So desperate became these struggles that I heard those near saying: "She is dying harder than any one I ever saw."

Standing beside her through it all was the great spirit whom I had heard say, "Take away the *cause* of the shadows" and he touched her troubled soul, speaking to it, spirit to spirit, and it struggled no longer but settled down in the resignation that comes only of such communion. Those watching about her thought the transition had come but instead she opened her eyes calmly to physical perceptions, then slept easily, peacefully, while the great Spirit remained, comforting her troubled soul, which had not altogether relinquished its desire to escape from its imprisonment of flesh while the bars of resistance were down.

Hours after she was lying wearily on the bed, awake, with the light gone out of her eyes and a great fear gripping her heart. When she would have taken comfort in the embraces of the old dream she found something cold and lifeless about it—an utter lack of responsiveness. It was then she turned to the doctor and whispered in a hoarse, croaking way:

"My voice—will it come back?"

"In time—yes," he made answer professionally, but she persisted:

"I mean—to sing?"

She saw the sentence in his eyes before his lips pronounced it:

"Possibly."

There was something—not the doctor—that told her the truth. She *knew* and turned her face to the wall, with her heart crying out, "Let me die—let me die," and later, in a half conscious way, with her face still to the wall, and her eyes closed, she was murmuring over and over again, "My soul is dead—my soul is dead."

There came another pause in this strange moving picture—the space was blank—and then I saw her taking up the burden of life in all its emptiness. Life and singing had been to her synonymous and now there was only life—the casket with the jewel gone. She despised life—it had become a great, empty waste and meant nothing to her. In the bitterness of it all she cried out: "There is no God," and a covering of materialism began weaving about the globe, which, still shadow-stained, enveloped her. The same Great Spirit looked on sorrowfully, respecting the law of self-responsibility and refrained from interference, yet was ever present with his protecting influence.

Then I saw her parents one after the other pass into the spirit world and she was alone, fighting that bitter fight; hating life, yet living. She felt that she was alone in the world but she was not. The same great spirit was with her always and when life's pitfalls yawned across her pathway, his hand ever held hers, lifting her safely over, preserving the white spotlessness of the globe where it had not been touched with the shadows which were growing dimmer and dimmer as the tragedies of life went on.

Then her heart was touched by something that had never come to it even in dreams, as ambition admitted no rivals. At last she knew the meaning of love, the splendor of which was so absorbing she felt it compensated for all that had been taken away—it was to her the "Land of Beginning Again," and life seemed to start all over with new promises, new ideals, such as ambition could never satisfy.

The great spirit smiled as though well pleased as he looked upon her new dream, but he did not leave her. He remained, helping her soul to grow yet stronger and teaching many lessons as though there was an object in view. She was not conscious of his presence and he seemed well content to have it so, seeming to know that when the time came for him to be recognized the way would be paved for her responsiveness.

Then came that well-remembered train scene. I saw her sitting there in perplexity, listening, wondering, while the great spirit was beside her. He had spoken and she had heard. Then he took her hand and she was conscious of his presence—it was *Meon.*

Then came the death scene—a scene of that very night, bringing earth existence down to the very end of its pilgrimage.

Naturally, regarding this as the end, I would have turned away but something compulsory in its strength held me. I looked about, half expecting to see *something* but to all appearances I was still alone —perhaps it was the shadow of earth's spiritual deafness and blindness that made me unable to see. Then I looked back where I had seen the "pictures" and was standing face to face with myself as a *spirit.* I looked at it and it looked at me. When this airy, fairy shadow form came and lay down at my feet in the attitude of restful relaxation, I was woefully perturbed. A moment later, quivering before my eyes was that same little light, larger and more illuminated, clothed with its wonderful globe radiance from which all the shadows were gone. It was glowing in unison with that same great *living* light essence in which it was incorporated, which interpenetrated everything. Then I looked down at the "shadow" body—the light was gone out of it!—Was it possible, —could it be *dead?* Being transparent, it seemed that I could see the deadness all through it and I shuddered, as I lifted my eyes again to the light that had deserted. It was still quivering within its wonderful illumination, then it slowly quivered upward and outward beyond the range of my vision. Again I looked upon the "dead" shadow body and shrank away from it, wondering, wondering—what could this mean? Did the "Shadow" body have to pass through the valley of death just as the physical did? In perplexity I turned away from it all and there stood Meon waiting. I would have told him what I had seen but he interrupted me evenly:

"I know."

"But why did you treat me like that, Meon?" I demanded.

"To build an edifice on the ashes," he answered impressively.

"And changed your mind?" almost sarcastically.

"No," with a touch of reproach that made me say hastily:

"Forgive me, Meon. What I saw made me live it all over again, the bitterness and the agony of it, but it does not matter now and I thank you for your interest."

"Now that you understand better the relationship of the earth plane and the *lives* after it, is it your desire to remain here or to return?"

"Return to earth," I replied unhesitatingly, rejoicing in this privilege which I felt would be mine, yet admitting that it was more than my worthiness justified.

"That is well," he said, as joined by many great souls who rejoiced with us, we descended into the environment which I has designated "the Power House;" and stood waiting.

"Come, tarry not, lest the gates of earth close against you," he admonished. "Are you ready?" I knew he meant the deterioration of the body and replied quickly: "I am," as I thought of what a catastrophe it would be, if after all, I returned to find the *brand* of death already upon my physical abode.

While I waited for Meon to lead the way—to go as we had come in—the floor seemed to give way and we went down with the sensation of falling through space.

CHAPTER XXIII.

MUNDANE READJUSTMENT.

I was trying to open my eyes, the lids of which had grown stiff and unyielding; trying to adjust myself in a case which seemed to have shrunken; trying to move hands that had grown heavy beyond my ability to lift. Meon and other spirits were hovering about me; I could feel the electrified essence, which had manifested its presence everywhere during my voyaging, drawing itself away—letting me go, as it were. Then the burden of physical life was full upon me and what a misfit I was! I felt as though I had been crammed into something several sizes too small for me. The heat within was awful while the exterior was cold and as heavy as lead.

While laboring in this agony of readjustment the nurse raised up, rubbing her eyes, with an expression of guiltiness on her face for having overslept:

"My how I have slept!" she was saying. "All night without waking; when have I done such a thing!"

Then she looked at me as though she had just thought of me and asked, trying to prune her voice to professional cadence:

"How are you this morning?"

"Very well, thank you," I managed to mumble as my benumbed tongue obeyed reluctantly the demand made upon it. Had she been less sleepy I am sure she would have noted the unusual sound of my voice, which was quaky and scarcely audible. Instead she yawned violently, drew herself up, got out of bed and went into the bathroom, leaving me thankful for the opportunity of further readjustment and examination of my exact physical status after existing for so long entirely independent of the body.

While she made her toilet I took the inventory. The finger nails were blue as though bruised. As I was unable to raise myself I could not see my toe nails but fancied that they were in the same condition and pushed them under the edge of the sheet and shut my hands so she could not see them and turned my face where it would be in shadow, all the time wondering how it looked. When I shut my hands I could not feel the nails on the palms and altogether there was such an unnatural feeling that I began investigating and of all disconcerting things it was the discovery that my body was insensible! How awesome was the thought of being a living soul in a dead body! I pinched myself, easily at first, then as vigorously as my limited strength would permit. This having no effect I took a hairpin, from where I had put it the night before when I loosened my hair, and with it pricked my arms, then my body through the thin gown but there was no more sensation than if I had been pricking the bed! It was terrible and I heard the nurse coming and closed my eyes. She came very near and after looking at me critically for a moment, remarked:

"Not eating is certainly telling on you."

Then it all came back, this sickening tragedy that seemed a thing of some other cycle of time, so much had happened since it had tortured me, and I had no time nor patience for it now, as the dead condition of my body was consuming all of my consideration. It was then when the very thought of eating was most hateful to me that breakfast was brought in, arranged in the daintiest and most tempting manner. I could have screamed at the sight of it, but restraining myself, I smiled and said pleasantly:

"I don't care for anything this morning, thank you."

After the tray had been taken away and the nurse's arguments over with, I again settled down to the perplexing problem confronting me. What ought I to do? After deliberating for a long time I called to the nurse:

"Will you please bring my rubber flesh brush from the bath room?"

When she returned with it, I said, by way of explanation:

"Thank you—my flesh seems so dead."

She looked at me disapprovingly and turned away without a word, as I began rubbing vigorously without producing the slightest effect. With the determination of *making* myself feel, I summed up all the strength I could and attacked my arm just below the elbow with a strenuousness that I did not realize until I felt the rubber working easily as though on damp flesh and looked at the arm to discover that the skin was removed and the blood oozing out, dampening the rubber. There was something sickening about it—so much so that my hands fell weak and helpless by my sides and the rubber rolled off on the floor. The nurse came over and picked it up and then brought a towel dipped in perfumed ice water and rubbed my face, which no doubt would have been refreshing if I could have felt it. I kept my arm in a position that hid the wound, shrinking from a questioning to which there was no satisfactory answer.

Then I realized that worrying was not helping me so what was the use of worrying? Plato tells us, "Nothing in human affairs is worth any great anxiety," and his philosophy is still our greatest exposition of idealism—in a speculative way. So I dismissed, or rather crowded out thoughts of my body by reviewing the occurrences of the night before and tried to formulate in my mind a working basis of all things being *one,* being interpenetrated by that wonderful magnetic or electrical current, invisible, silent, powerful. Finally the illustration that most appealed to me was likening it to an electric power house to which we are as the lights in the different parts of the city, each with its own scope of illumination, a power that can be turned on or off at will. Connected it illuminates our own pathway and those of others, if turned off we grope as blind creatures, crying out in the darkness. But we cannot get away from this silent invisible power; it is always there, to be used or abused as we elect.

How wonderful it all was and yet I dared not even hint it to any one, despite the fact that we have reached that stage of progression where we recognize nothing as impossible, using every day commonplace things which were once high among recognized impossibilities. Suppose for instance some one had told our forefathers, as they rubbed stones together to produce a light, that the time would come when by touching a tiny button a whole building or city would be lighted up instantly—that a man could sit in Washington and press a button that would light up a skyscraper in New York or anywhere else on this continent and that in future, the same could be done anywhere in the world. When they were killing their horses riding in mad haste to deliver messages suppose some one had suggested that the time would be when a message could circle the globe before they could saddle the horse; could they then have believed that a person could sit in one city and converse with another miles away; could they foresee the wonders of wireless telegraphy—and that the same principle will in time be applied to telephony? Take moving pictures for instance—suppose some misguided wretch had suggested years ago that anyone could play in New York and be seen by the whole world; further, that the player dying would make no difference—he or she could play on and could be seen after death just the same as before. Similarly in the case of a phonograph record—it is not altered in the least by the death of the singer—technically we hear the dead sing—see the dead play, but there is nothing supernatural about it. It is that great silent invisible force ELECTRICITY demonstrating its power on earth at it does in the invisible spheres. We have made all these wonderful things common by everyday use and so we will go ever onward filling the wonders of today with the commonplaces of tomorrow, and there are many wonders still unborn, greater even then we dream.

Spirit communication is one of the wonders of today that tomorrow will claim for its commonplaces, when we will converse with the so-called dead as easily as we now do with the living; communicate with other realms as we now do other cities; visit the invisible worlds, leaving our physical bodies at home just as we now do our other material possessions.

Really spirit communication is nothing new—it is as old as the records of the world; all religion is based on it; without it there would be no religious foundation, nothing on which to hang the theory of "life after death." While *conscious* continuity of life has been admitted down through the ages, evidence of it has always been shrouded in mystery and uncertainty—a glaring inconsistency—but the time is now upon us when it refuses to be denied any longer and insists on taking its place in the foremost ranks of demonstrated facts. It is a demonstrated fact, admitted by the greatest scientists and thinkers of the world, who see the "handwriting on the wall" that all who will may read and understand.

The history of spirit communion is rather diversified, as each age had treated it in its own way whether right or wrong. In Biblical times those who communed with spirits were sacred, the chosen of God; in later days they were burned at the stake as witches, heretics and worse; still later they were incarcerated within asylums for the insane; but now it has met us at Philippi—we stand face to face with it, with no choice but acceptance; and still later, in the future, it will revolutionize the world. There will be peace, one nation, one religion and we will wonder how it could ever have been otherwise. However, there is a price, a mighty toll, to be paid before this ideal condition prevails.

How I digress!

I could not chain my thoughts to earth that day; they would soar away and I seemed to live in that far away world, away from the earth and all of its sordidness, but when the lunch hour came it dragged me down again to that everlasting eating tragedy—the war of the seen and unseen over a soul that belonged to neither and yet to both—one exacting a fast, the other a feast. The nurse had reached the limit of her patience and a few minutes later I heard her phoning the doctor, admitting her inability to "cope with such contrariness."

About the middle of the afternoon the doctor came and after exhausting his power of persuasion, delivered the following ultimatum:

"You will either eat or be sent where the operation will be performed under compulsory conditions."

I flinched under such a lash but made no appeal. After he had gone, however, I cried pleadingly to the forces that held me, cried out into the invisible void, "be merciful," but no answering voice came back and I knew that until I was released the fast would prevail regardless of consequences. But was there such a place where people could be made to eat whether they wanted to or not? Was he trying to frighten me into compliance?

I asked myself lots of questions and was very unhappy for a while and then utterly weary of the tragedy of it all—of watching preparations go forward in accordance with the doctor's ultimatum, of the bitterness of it all, I turned my face to the wall. Tears that hurt as they moistened the dry benumbed lids came sparingly as though the parched lids absorbed them before they could escape. Then a peace came upon me—I did not care—nothing mattered. No matter how the tide ebbed I would just drift with it in utter disregard. I would make no appeal where either world was concerned, they could do with me as they liked. Suddenly I realized that I was exceedingly hungry and thirsty and there was a stinging sensation in the throat. It needed no one to tell me that I had been released. I knew it before I heard the voice saying:

"Eat—drink."

Now that the *fasting pressure* was lifted a strange regret, almost apprehensive, came upon me and I was wondering if the spiritual privileges had been entirely withdrawn and I had been unreservedly given back to the physical. Though hungry and thirsty I remained for some time as I was, loath to dissipate a condition that had played its part in the *transitional* drama of the night before, the memory of which seemed even more beautiful than the reality. I had wanted to come back to earth but now was I altogether satisfied that I had done so?

A special dinner was prepared that evening and served with as much ceremony as though in reality it celebrated my return from the "Port of Missing Men," all of which I appreciated more than I dared express, feigning an indifference the absence of frankness enforced. However, I ate very sparingly, as someway, I was not really hungry when the time came but it satisfied those interested and that was much.

At last the long day with its mundane and supermundane exactions was over and I was alone in the night watches again, wondering if I had been given back unreservedly to the mundane and was almost afraid to call into the silence lest I should find it void, a confirmation more terrible than suspense. As I waited in this awful uncertainty, I perceived Meon beside me, felt the great electrified current envelop me, and before I fully realized what was transpiring, I was again riding on the vibratory waves of space.

CHAPTER XXIV.

MUNDANE AND SUPERMUNDANE RELATIONSHIP.

"That which was profitable to the soul of man the Father revealed to the ancients; that which is profitable to the soul of man today revealeth He this day."

Again I looked down upon my vacated body but it was not nearly so interesting as it had been the night before, and after the most casual observation I vibrated leisurely about within the environment of the earth, wondering what was forthcoming.

For some time I waited for Meon to speak but as he did not, I ventured:

"Where are we going, Meon?"

"Would you care to observe the earth in its actual relationship with the invisible?"

"Nothing would please me more," I assured him, feeling almost enthusiastic at the prospect.

"Come," he called and we vibrated lower upon the face of the earth where the vibrations became more pronounced, as we harmonized with its magnetism.

I floated easily about over the city, taking what might be termed a physical inventory. I wanted to see if things looked the same viewed from the other side of life. They did. Moonlight flooded the city with its softness and I looked into the faces of the stars, feeling the witchery of the night's perfection much as I had always done; the automobiles, conveyances, pedestrians, were hurrying along just as usual. The buildings and everything looked just the same.

The "town clock" was nearing the midnight hour. After looking into its familiar face a few seconds, I turned away and would have walked upon the sidewalk that I might go into the buildings through their doors but Meon entered easily through the wall, and with just a little misgiving I followed and learned that material constructions or obstructions formed no bar to my sight or passing. I was surprised that I had not thought of that before as it seemed I must have known it, as otherwise how could I have gone out and come in the night before?

As the inhabitants lay wrapped in the oblivion of sleep we passed into their homes, even unto the most sacred firesides and stood aghast as the doors of skeleton closets creaked on their rusty hinges and strange ghosts walked out in full view, concealing nothing; nothing could be concealed as between souls there can be no deceptions. Those of us who spend our energies making deception and concealment fine arts find in the end how worse than useless has been the expenditure of our energies. How strange it all seemed as we violated home after home, passing through the "halls of pleasure," and the "isles of pain," until I began to feel ashamed of the unfair advantage I was taking of unsuspecting and defenseless humanity and would have returned but Meon spurred me to renewed activity by saying solemnly:

"One must first procure knowledge before giving it—to serve humanity one must know humanity."

And thus using my purpose to excuse my act, I went on and on, suspended above or standing by the bedside of the sleeping, conversing with the soul that never sleeps. In fact, in some instances souls were entirely absent from the bodies as they slept, away somewhere. When I first observed that sleep is nothing more nor less than the soul leaving the body for the higher pleasures and benefits of the spirit world I was shocked but soon became accustomed to seeing disembodied spirits and spirits of the sleeping mingling together in the friendliest and most natural manner.

The "household" or guardian spirits in some homes objected to our entry and we passed on, respecting the objection without question, as some spirits love the human beings over whom they keep watch so devotedly that they exclude from them all other spirit influence or interference. Such protection other spirits respect as long as the human beings thus guarded make no objections, and as most persons are unconscious of invisible solicitude they neither appreciate it nor object to it. In some instances it is all right but in others it would be better to break the influence. However, this breaking up or changing ones invisible household is a very serious matter and should be undertaken only with discriminating intellectuality and spirituality, or even more undesirable entities may enter into the vacancy created by the departure of those who must retire at the command of the one concerned. While the law of "like attracts like," is excellent, we must not lose sight of the fact that "a chain is no stronger than its weakest link" and that we are no stronger than our weakest propensity.

> "And good may ever conquer ill
>   Health walk where pain has trod
> 'As a man thinketh so he is'
>   Arise and think with God."

Varied were the emotions born within me as I viewed uncovered souls and knew them as they knew themselves in all their sin-laden weariness and sorrow-laden memories. Even the whitest and purest souls suffer because of fancied sins even more than real criminals suffer for real crimes. Even little children sorrow deeply, as I saw little pillows damp with childish tears that aching hearts had pumped to the surface—a soul as old as time struggling with a new opportunity. Selfishness enthroned itself in many hearts while the willing subjects held unto themselves the joy of self-love which poisons while it pleases. There were blackened souls within handsome and beautiful bodies of men and women; souls too pure and white for earth's tragedies incorporated within weak, deformed and ugly bodies; then there were beautiful souls within beautiful bodies; hideous souls within hideous bodies, and so it went on and on, the invisible influence ever in evidence. Some otherwise beautiful souls were held in unconscious bondage by invisible earth-magnetized beings whose influence was worse than degrading, even criminal. It is such influence that sometimes make criminals after committing a most revolting crime defend their actions by claiming that "God" or some scion among the influential dead told them to do it. They feel perfectly justified in what they have done regardless of consequences to themselves or any one else. Such earth-magnetized spirits live, in a way, the physical life, at the expense of human beings, and in some way gather unto themselves strength beyond the average spirit, so much so that they can imitate the voice or appearance of any person they find it expedient to represent. They find some person of their own instincts and dominate him and when he is sufficiently sensitive for the purpose for which he has been trained, they appear to him, or speak assuming the appearance or voice of the person most effective in the accomplishment of their design. They assist in the accomplishment of crime, as well as in the apprehension of the criminal, rejoicing in the chain of misery they have the power to create as well as to satisfy their craving to identify themselves with physical action. St. Paul warns us:

"Beloved, believe not every spirit but try the spirits whether they are of God."

Reason was given us to use, therefore, we should put the search light of reason on everything, spiritual as well as material. No matter what comes from the invisible world submit it to the highest pressure of *reason* before becoming identified with it or acting in accordance with it. Spirits are only disembodied human beings, who take human frailties and perversities into the spirit world with them, some having a very hard time ridding themselves of them. We retain our identity absolutely as we would not be *ourselves* if by simply coming out of our physical bodies we changed immediately into a soul much better or infinitely worse. What we are in this world is what we will be when we "wake up and find ourselves dead" and so we shall remain until, by our own spiritual strength, we evolve into the higher conditions of the after life. However, it is possible for us to so live while in the earth life that we may pass unconsciously through all eliminating conditions, and wake in what one might term the Heaven World, a condition of extreme spiritual happiness. Very few go by way of this direct route.

I cannot too strongly impress it upon the reader that there are no *lost* souls. The unfortunate creatures who go into the spirit world after abusing, through their own weakness, the privilege of earth life, fall out of the evolutionary vibrations for a time and become creatures of retrogression instead of progression but sooner or later that ever onward irresistible current takes them within itself and unifies them with the great scheme of things. We may give this class our pity and our prayers but we must shut them out of communion with us until we have attained soul strength sufficient to uplift them instead of being degraded by them. In fact, they are very good things to leave alone entirely until we are quite sure of ourselves. We must learn to *know* that nothing can make us evil or commit criminal acts against our wills—nothing can really hurt us but *ourselves*. There is a "still small voice" within which we call "conscience" and which never fails. When in doubt we should just listen to it. Listening, we cannot act wrong and feel happy in so doing.

So I floated on and on over the sleeping city, listening and learning, earth life an open book before me. I floated through the iron bars into the jail and looked down with pity noting that there were souls not nearly so shadow stained as many who were free. Poor dominated creatures, miserable and pliant in their unconscious servitude, I wanted to tell them how easy it would be to shake off such influence and be free but not one heard me, although I persisted in calling. One young man, a sailor, turned quickly and listened when I called but that was all. Although the hour was late he was sitting, staring out of the window; he turned his face, listened a moment then sighed and stared on. He was thinking of his home and loved ones across the sea, and I could see the little home and all of its details, his mind imaged it so perfectly.

Then I went down on the wharves, into the ships and every ship had its individual invisible household, that seemed to belong to it as much as the furniture or even the material with which it was built. These spirits seemed to be much happier in every way than those who confine themselves upon the land. Instead of making objections to my coming among them they welcomed me more cordially than any other class that I had intruded my presence upon. It was really like a social diversion. They talked freely, explaining many things of interest. They accompanied me out upon the wharves but in no instance did they enter a ship other than their own.

When I was back upon the land rather a pitiable condition manifested itself to me. There were souls who could not realize that they were dead and imagined themselves still in the earth life. One was excessively unhappy because of being ignored by friends and loved ones. He could see and hear them but they could not hear him speak nor see him. Not knowing that he was dead he could not understand why. Some were groping about, ever feeling, as though they could not see, calling in the most pitiful, pleading way, "Where are you?—where are you?" as though searching for some one they could not find, with the name dearest to them ever on their lips. I realized what a dreadful thing it was to live in the spirit world recognizing only the physical, ignoring the soul, shutting it out from the growth and development which is the purpose of the earth existence and the reason it is given to us. I shuddered and turned away from this condition, to one, if anything, more uncanny; there were souls sleeping—peacefully enough—but just sleeping in the darkness—waiting —waiting for what? A call to awaken them, or had they just dropped out to peacefully await another cycle of time? Those who slept were certainly not unhappy, but just sleeping "even as you and I."

I had grown weary of seeing things I did not care to see and turned my eyes away, shutting out all sights, wondering if there was nothing beautiful in the relationship of the seen and unseen. So far my observations had been rather disappointing, and I felt inclined to go back into my body if what I had seen was all there was to our invisible relationship. When I would have made this suggestion to Meon I observed that everything was changed, even the vibrations were different. I could feel the interpenetration of that great electrified current, see the light of it spreading out over everything. Great souls were coming down through the darkness illuminating as they came down the electrified pathway between the earth and the higher planes. While these beings do not directly interfere with the law of "self-responsibility," which requires each soul to choose for itself between right and wrong, their influence has much to do with the choosing, as well as in the rectifying when the wrong choice has been made, each soul paying the price its wrong choice involves.

Almost every one is, at times, consciously or unconsciously en rapport with these highly evolved souls, as they harmonize with the mundane strata and leave permanent creations in the form of art, literature, music, love—things that make life worth while to us. There is a note within every human being in tune with the infinite and we must sometimes feel it when the chord is struck. Sometimes we are conscious of it when we stand in the presence of a masterpiece of nature or of man. At such times a memory, a chord or strain of music touches within and stabs us, as it were, with something too deep and exquisite to analyze, leaving a sense of something higher—illusive though it may be—something, somewhere—the soul-touch of higher things.

There is another class of spirits that seem to belong, in rather a permanent way, to the invisible world about us. They are not highly evolved and know practically nothing about the world beyond this but they seem to be helpers and friends to humanity, doing all they can to make the earth life happier. They are very happy and companionable themselves, laughing and playing like children amongst us all the time. Nor are they above playing harmless pranks and jokes on us, which give them much amusement and do not harm us. They are more attracted and helpful to some persons than others, as some seem to attract while others repel them. Their position does not seem to be an important one but they keep life from being too burdensomely serious by adding to it a touch of humor and playfulness. They go down under the earth which is very easy of access to them and to a certain extent in the air, confining themselves, however, very closely within the area of human habitation. They have names which are very unlike the earth variety but rather pretty. While I have never attended a spiritualistic seance of any kind I fancy these spirits would lend themselves quite unreservedly to such occasions and do all they could to promote communication between the two worlds but if they presided over it entirely there would be little to learn further than the possibility of such communication. The mere fact that such communication is possible, however, is much to the investigator.

Then came a phase so tender and beautiful that I looked on almost reverently. It was the tender solicitude of departed loved ones.

There was the good, pure spirit mother watching lovingly over her children, especially the little ones whom her transition had left at the mercy of the world. I saw her bending with hopeful persuasion over the wayward son, pleading with him who heeded her not. There was the loving, protecting father helping and comforting the child that needed him most, teaching the one most vulnerable to his influence; innocent little children were kissing the lips of their sleeping parents, murmuring "Mama—Papa;" there was the loving husband or wife, trying to lighten burdens that weighed heavily on beloved shoulders and impress his or her presence on the object of solicitude. Friends came to friends; loved ones to loved ones. Eyes looked tenderly into eyes that saw them not; voices went lovingly into ears that heard them not; lips pressed lips that felt them not.

"Eyes watch us that we cannot see
    Lips warn us that we may not kiss
They wait for us and starrily
    Lean towards us from Heaven's lattices."

The beauty of all this was that these souls were not bound by the magnetism of the earth but by the ties of love, which transition glorified, making it a pure, holy offering, compared to which love in the earth life is only a shadow. They come and go at will. Yet, I strongly advise those investigating this subject or any one who passes into a condition of *sensitiveness* sufficient to communicate with the invisible, not to call too often to the loved ones on the other side, as they have their lives there with its attending duties of progression, which demand much of them. The refining of the soul is a delicate process which interference complicates. If they care to come of their own volition it is well; let them understand that you are always glad to have them come when they will. I looked upon some beautiful souls that were held almost earth-bound by the continuous and selfish calling of loved ones still in the earth life who could not even recognize them when they came and were regardless of the sacrifices they were causing. When it is possible for our loved ones to come they will do so without our exacting it. On the other hand such exactions without the possibility of compliance leave us open to spirits of deception who would gladly embrace the opportunity of representing themselves to be the desired one. As we are prone to believe without question what our loved ones tell us, we thereby risk putting ourselves in the power of unscrupulous spirits. Those who have learned discrimination run no such risks; it is the beginner who should be careful.

Another interesting phase of this wheels-within-wheels, mundane-supermundane conglomeration was that of persons who had passed out of life with unfinished work to which they had devoted their lives and talents. They were seeking earnestly for "sensitives" vulnerable to their influence. When such a "receiving station" is found they help and direct without dominating the continuance of their achievements and labors, to which is added the knowledge that the evolution to a higher existence supplies—one of the greatest forces in earth's progress. Many of our great men are still living amongst us in this way. Instead of going on the journey of individual progression they are sacrificing themselves on the altar of progression of humanity in general, which in the end will be a sacrifice more than well made.

As I went on taking soul inventories over the city I came near unto my fiance but loyalty placed her white hands over my soul's eyes and I passed on without the slightest desire of "seeing unseen" any skeletons that might darken his closet—if there were any they were, to me, too sacred to violate. This, however, did not apply to his friends, so I vibrated out to the home of one of his business associates and floated through the walls into his presence. He was surrounded by highly evolved beings, who while they loved him very much made not the slightest objection to my coming as near to him as I desired. He recognized my presence immediately as that of a spirit, an unseen thing, without recognizing who it was. I was shocked to see suspended over his head a scroll so nearly unwound that it was hanging by the merest thread, vibrating, quivering, threatening to "let go" as I looked. It needed no one to tell me that this soul was preparing to "raise anchor" for other seas.

When I would have told him, would have warned him of his coming transition, I perceived that he knew it and was arranging his business affairs accordingly. As I looked upon his soul splendor I realized how erroneous is the teaching against the spiritual greatness of a rich man. He was rich unquestionably in material possessions but richer still in soul achievement and spiritual strength. In the consciousness of his impending transition I remained for some time studying this phase of life's drama and then left the room wrapped in that awed reverence we feel in the presence of approaching "death."

The next day I told my fiance of this coming transition but he chided me for "foolish fancies" but I knew different—a difference which a few weeks verified.

When I was again suspended over the city I bathed listlessly in the moonlight, listening to the moaning of the sea, with all desire for further delving into the soul problem gone. It was all such a tangled web, so many conflicting influences and contradictory manifestations that I felt it was a problem stupendous beyond my ability to solve—a veritable puzzle. Really there was no happiness. There was no soul however shadowed by sin that sorrow did not outweigh the sin, even in those who "combine one virtue with a thousand crimes." In the midst of my conjectures I noted a strange shadow-like darkness, creeping upon the earth, enveloping it and such a wave of tragedy and unhappiness swept over me that I was almost afraid. I turned with the thought of running back into my body but the darkness was terrible and I heard a voice saying: "Earth is a giant Gethsemane," and so it seemed, as I waited, wondering.

Then I felt the great electrified current and my distress vanished instantly. I could see it spreading out, far out over the face of the earth dispelling the darkness, consuming the sorrow. Everything was transformed, transfigured, and looking up I saw the "Power House" as though it were very near and great was the illumination between. As I looked suddenly I beheld a face that we all know and heard voices crying out:

"Behold the second coming of Christ."

Slowly this vision faded and I was looking down on the uncovered souls of the city just as though there had been no insert of agonizing darkness followed by the light and its wonderful promise. So much had been crowded into such a limited period of time that there was a sense of confusion and uncertainty in the midst of which I appealed to Meon:

"Meon, I want to go back—I am so tired that fancy is taking liberties with me."

"Very well, but to accuse Fancy is not to convict it."

"But *is* Christ coming to earth again?"

"Certainly," he replied impressively. "The reincarnation of this great teacher by a perfectly natural and recognized law is soon to be fulfilled."

Further questioning availed little and when I would have escaped into my body as into a refuge I observed beside it a spirit woman crouching furtively, her hands grasping frantically trying to touch it, her eyes gleaming, her face passionate with eagerness, showing how vitally intent she was upon her purpose whatever it was. I turned to Meon for explanation:

"What is she doing?" I asked mystified.

"Trying to appropriate your body during your absence," he replied evenly, filling me with apprehension, which he allayed by adding: "But she wont

—she cannot even touch it. It is protected against invasions of all kinds."

Looking up she saw us and with a screeching, moaning cry she slunk away in the darkness. The echoes of her piteous moans wafted back, making even the "flesh" of my soul "creep." I gazed after her intently even after I could no longer see nor hear her, conjecturing. Then suddenly I was aghast at the revelation, feeling that I had solved the mystery of "lost identity," which has so baffled our physicians and scientists.

Then I slipped into my body and readjusted myself much more easily than I had the night before.

All souls leave their bodies at times consciously or unconsciously, always during sleep, which is only a matter of the soul (or spirit) leaving the body and going out into the spirit world. When it returns we "wake up." Why do we not bring back the consciousness of such experiences? Really I do not know. What I do *know* is that souls are out of their bodies during sleep for I saw this to be a fact. Some were near their bodies, others were nowhere to be seen, evidently on journeys into higher realms. However, during this time the bodies are protected against piracy of the earth magnetized beings, who would be glad to appropriate any body in order to function in the earth life. Because of this splendid system of protection such cases are fortunately exceedingly rare. It is a very interesting subject none the less. I recall reading recently of a case where even the eyes and the stature had changed. The fact is, it is an entirely different soul that inhabits the body. Possibly the former incumbent deserted its earth abode for joys of other realms leaving it at the mercy of the merciless. Possibly some disembodied spirit gained strength superior to the embodied and simply ejected it. Too, I believe this change has been made by spirits so conversant with the affairs of the person in question that no one ever suspected it. There are cases where persons have changed in character so suddenly and entirely that no accepted theory could reasonably explain them. There are, I believe, instances where the rightful owner has, after a time, regained possession of its earth abode and remembers nothing of the transaction, or so claims. The chances are that he does not. On the other hand Public Opinion (the tyrant that makes or mars the average life) would curtail frankness in the matter. This also could be applied to insanity.

This, however, was not the only time I saw that woman and heard her wailings. At times while within my body I felt her disturbing presence, which was always heralded by an unaccountable attack of what we call the "blues." Then I strengthened myself against her influence, mentally affirming that she could not affect me in any way, that I was superior to such influence. After that when she came there was only the consciousness of her sinladen and sorrowing presence. I pitied her and spoke to her kindly, asking her to leave me, which she always did immediately but as she went the moaning cries that floated back pierced my heart with a pity that was painful.

Later she came and seemed more comforted. Her cries became less and less agonizing, and her presence less disturbing.

At last she came—it was a soft, breeze-laden summer's night as I lay in convalescense. I perceived her presence and knew she stood beside the bed but as she had never spoken, I did not even listen. Then she came very near—nearer than she had ever come before and whispered pleadingly:

"Let me touch your hand, please."

I lifted my hand that she might take it if she so desired and as her icy touch came upon it she bent over me and said with passionate earnestness:

"Oh, beautiful soul, through you I have seen the truth and the light and I go toward them blessing you."

With all my weaving of dreams, all the promises that passing behind the veil had given, I had never considered the possibility of helping a soul that had passed beyond the mundane, while I was still in the mundane life, and yet, why not? While still marveling at the revelation she passed out of my presence and has never since returned.

CHAPTER XXV.

THE LINK OF INFINITUDE.

The next day was dreary, melancholy and the mood was contagious, especially when as the afternoon wore on, rain drizzled with a plaintive, pattering sound on the metal roof, distant thunder rolled and a rough sea was roaring and moaning as the waves dashed on the rocks beyond the seawall. A fitting background for depression. Then the rain poured down with the steadiness that promises to last several hours and I listened to the downpour with a vague sense of unhappiness. Tears came and went spasmodically as that "what is the use?" feeling pressed upon me. The conviction that I was going to die was a thing not to be shaken off; I argued that one could not live who was already dead. I realized that while out of my body I lived with the so-called dead—that my body was only a place where I "kept up appearances" of being alive during the day but when night came I deserted it for the real life—the life in the spirit world. I felt that all my hopes and dreams had been foolish—out of all reason—and that there was nothing for me to do but just die and be done with it—just go out and never return.

I knew it was impossible for this condition to last much longer. It seemed that I was more illy adjusted than usual, my body was a thing painfully apart from me. I could consciously recognize myself as two separate entities. The outer or physical was cold with the heaviness of clay, while the soul or inner was light and strong, resenting the prison walls in which it was confined.

Then I perceived Meon beside me and complained:

"When this sensitiveness came upon me I was in perfect health and strength, why have I been otherwise since?"

"A condition necessary for what had transpired and is still to transpire."

"Tell me, please, am I to remain on earth or am I going to die? This has become unbearable."

"It will not be required much longer," he replied, looking at me reproachfully, but I persisted:

"But you have not answered my question."

"It will answer itself soon enough."

This disturbing unrest was still upon me when my Beloved came in the evening and I welcomed the diversion he offered. Opening a book he said:

"I have brought the Rubayat of Omar Khayyam to read to you—would you like it?"

"Surely yes—it will be like old times," I assured him as I thought almost regretfully of the mysterious force that had come into my life touching its rifting fingers to the perfect lute of our comradeship.

Every word of the quaint Bacchanalian philosophy was like a return of an old friend who had been long absent and as he read ever and anon he would lift his eyes to mine in appreciation of my undivided attention and the congeniality of our literary tastes.

When he came to this:

I sent my soul through the Invisible
    Some letter of that after life to spell
And by and by my soul returned to me
    And answered, "I myself am Heaven and Hell."

How forcibly the truth of it struck me! All of life's philosophy summed up in one little sentence! No matter what we say, what we do, or where we go, there are means of escaping everything but just *ourselves,* and from ourselves there is no escape in this life nor the life to come, even unto the end of the journey, therefore, it is well to make of *ourselves,* our most desirable companions, for it is this companionship that will outlast all things else, even throughout all eternity.

He was quick to note my abstraction and said with apologetic solicitude:

"I have wearied you reading so long but it seemed so good to have you listen again."

"I am not tired. It is such a pleasure—." I hastened to assure him, but he closed the book saying:

"We will take no chances—there will be days and days we can read together when you are well."

"You are considerate to a fault," I said, half laughing, trying to disguise my regret that the reading was over.

After he had gone for some time the magnetism of his presence lingered, preventing an immediate return to the despondency that the day had fastened upon me, but it was not long before the duet of the rain and sea made me restless again and I called into the silence. No answering voice came. No loneliness that afflicts mortals is greater than that caused by the withdrawal of the companionship of the spirit world, after one has experienced the joys of it. I turned again to the dismal earth sounds and complained that sleep, "nature's soft nurse," refused to come while I was still within the domain of her comforting influence, feeling that by another night I would be entirely and forever removed from its necessity. As though accepting the challenge she folded me tenderly to her bosom, lifting me above the melancholia that had so dominated my waking hours.

I was awakened by thousands of spirit voices blending in a monotonous chant, the same thing over and over again. With one voice they chanted one sentence and that sentence was: "Thy will be done, O God, not mine." Some of the voices were sweet and low; some high and loud; some near; some came from afar, yet there was no discord but perfect monotonous harmony, if one can conceive of a thing so rare. After listening to it for some time wondering why they made no variation in voice or word, I tried to shut it out and go back to sleep but I reckoned without the chanters, who, with renewed energies put sleep in the category of impossibilities.

After resenting it awhile I tried to harmonize my soul with the sentiment, and to join in the spirit of it but some way my "old self" seemed to have come back and resentment kindled anew. I argued that my *will* is mine to use, not to make it subjective to that of another, even though it were God's and that I would use it just as I elected. Thus my resentment grew in pace with the ever increasing power and persistence of the monotonous chanting, which finally became so nerve-racking that I felt like running out into the street, into the rain—anywhere to escape it—as it went on and on and on, no faster no slower, just dead level monotony.

When it seemed I could endure it no longer, I called Meon but as no response came I called for just any one who would answer with the determination of coming to some understanding, or even compromise if necessary—anything if they would only stop demanding that which was expected of me. Naturally this attempted communication threw me more intimately into their vibration, which almost overpowered me with their sentiment that I should join in the chant not only in words but in sentiment, but I did not succumb. However, I could feel my resentment wearing itself out, my arguments seemed weak and unsustained. I was tired—utterly weary—and I wanted them to just please hush, if only for a moment. The clock struck two and I remember wishing it was twelve and in fancy I almost felt the thrill of counting twelve big, long strokes as they hammered into the monotony. Instead the two little strokes had come and gone and my soul was pleading "please hush" into the very silence, which the voices so violated.

Then in a vague dream-like way, I caught the faintest glimpse of the mantle of "Self-Responsibility" just as I had seen it come fluttering down upon me in the panorama of my earth lift. Suddenly I was stabbed, as it were, with the realization that accepting this was not compulsory but was, in reality, the greatest of all privileges being offered for my acceptance or rejection—the privilege of thinking with God. I realized that by merging my will in the Universal Will its power would be my power and the prerogative would be mine of thinking and acting in *conscious* oneness with the All-Intelligence, that instead of making my will subjective such a unification would give it a dominance that it could not otherwise attain.

I was appalled at my stupidity in resisting this privilege and wondered how I could have been so blind. Yes, it was the law of Self-Responsibility in operation. My choice had been left absolutely uninfluenced. Even now I wondered what would have been the result had I rejected it. Just to think that while clothed in the authority of Self-Responsibility, wrapped in my garment of flesh within the magnetism of earth, I had persistently resisted that which I most ardently sought when beyond earth's confines —conscious *oneness* with all power. How unworthy I felt as I listened to the offering of the privilege of privileges, feeling that no matter to what extent a soul may progress, as long as it remains on earth it is assailed by diverse influences. Finally I shook it all off and took refuge in the joy that I had not entirely succumbed and began harmonizing myself with the prevailing sentiment, preparatory to its acceptance.

Although the dawn was bathing the room in gray the chanters kept on and on. It was no longer dreary monotony but the sweetest music I had ever heard. Tears of contrition, hot and blinding, came into my eyes as a link came down into my soul chaining me to the Infinite, unifying my will with the Great Will, as my soul in uplifting exultation, softened by humility, lifted up its voice in unison with the chanters in words and sentiment; "Thy will be done, O God, not mine."

Slowly the chanting merged into a magnificent rendition—the most wonderful thing I have ever heard—thousands of voices singing as only spirit voices can to the accompaniment of the Choir invisible, in which my soul joined, a living, vibrating responsive chord.

Then came silence spreading wings of peaceful

calm over everything and although the day had come, the fringed curtains of my eyes came down, shutting out the light, and I passed into the unconsciousness which is one of the most beautiful provisions in the whole scheme of things.

CHAPTER XXVI.

ATOMS OF LIFE UNIFYING WITH THE SOURCE OF LIFE.

I was awakened by the bringing of the breakfast tray and as it sat before me a voice said:

"Eat nothing—drink nothing."

"Oh, surely that tragedy is not to be reenacted," I protested.

"Just for today."

Closing my eyes I sent the breakfast away saying:

"I would rather sleep," and sleep I did until a voice came calling me into wakefulness with the injunction:

"Exercise today the privilege you accepted last night."

My mind went back and reviewed all that had happened during the night. I seemed to live it all over again, analyzing it, repeating, "Thy will be done, O God, not mine." I realized that it did not mean the negation of *your* will or *my* will but the uplifting of our consciousness into cooperative oneness with the Universal or God Will, of which our wills are an individualized manifestation. This for the reason that in the final analysis there is but one will, to which we are as drops of water to the sea, grains of sand to the land. Truly:

"All are parts of one stupendous whole
Whose body nature is and God the soul."

Conscious co-operation or conscious *oneness* with the God *Will* can only be acquired by exercising and strengthening what we recognize as *our* wills in an individualized way, with the consciousness of our unity with the God will, which will be powerful individually only according to the strength we inject into it. First we must *know* we are right, on which point the "still small voice" within will keep us advised. Then armed with the golden rule and generosity in everyday affairs, let nothing swerve us from our real purposes.

As the day wore on I seemed to live further and further away from the earth, so much so that its requirements grated on me and human voices seemed unnatural, loud and harsh. I therefore kept my eyes closed that the nurse might fancy me asleep and refrain from speaking or disturbing me in any way. The deadness of my body weighed heavily upon me and I had the sensation of having something cold and heavy wrapped around me. When my hands closed they seemed to hold some foreign substance in them; even sight grew dim, so dim that objects in the spirit world were more discernible than those in the room. Above all was the conviction that at last the time had come to close the book of my physical existence, not to be reopened during the present cycle of time and it mattered little one way or the other. I was just drifting, trying to keep in tune with the Infinite, bolstering myself up with the supplication "Unify my soul with thy purpose, O God," feeling that if this "purpose" was for me to remain on earth I would, otherwise I would not.

Not eating caused little comment, as I promised that while I did not feel like eating today I would tomorrow whether I felt like it or not. "Tomorrow —tomorrow never comes," kept reiterating itself until it seemed I had already passed over the borderland and there was a tomorrow—the tomorrow of death—life everlasting. Thus a kind of semi-consciousness began playing its part in the drama and I was glad when

> "I saw night
> Digging the grave of day
> And day take off her golden crown
> And flung it sorrowfully down."

Later I mechanically watched the nurse performing her little ante-slumber duties, feeling that the same duties would not be required of her when night came again. Then she crept into bed noiselessly and was soon asleep and I was knocking at the door of the Silence from which no answer came. I knew, however, that I was not alone, as my soul felt that unmistakable comfort of soul companionship and I just waited listlessly.

When I was almost weary of waiting, weary of everything, I perceived Meon beside me and asked eagerly:

"Oh, Meon, am I coming out tonight? I am so weary of earth."

"Yes, come," he made answer and I almost jumped out of my body so eager was I to escape and I soon vibrated far out into the soft whiteness of the Space-World, happier and more carefree than I had ever been before.

As I vibrated onward I noted the similarity of the vibrations to those of a moving train and asked:

"Meon, did the vibrations of that moving train have anything to do with facilitating your first communication?"

"Yes, by throwing you en rapport with these vibrations."

"But I was not thinking of such things," I protested.

"Which still further facilitated matters."

"I was reading, if you remember."

"No; you were not *reading*—you were looking over the paper with your mentality open to receive the most unexpected intelligence, creating an ideal condition. I spoke—you heard."

As we drifted far out, ever onward, I noted with interest great vibrating orbs of light and remember wondering if they were inhabited to which Meon vouchsafed the intelligence that they were and the desire was strong upon me to visit them. In a moment, however, this impulse was blotted out by the beauty of the "scenery," as we vibrated onward through the cloud mountains of space, quivering within the electrified current as a part of it; colors mingled and intermingled suggesting rainbows bathing in a silvery sea—the silvery sea whose waves seemed propelling us and thousands of others ever onward toward a wonderful shore somewhere in a wonderful world.

Almost abruptly we were upon a substantial whiteness which I instantly recognized as "The Power House of Existence." I realize it is a liberty on my part to presume to name this plane of existence as it doubtless has a name already, but as I designate it according to its functions, it would not interfere with its position as a numerical plane, which I am quite sure it is, as there are a number of planes or phases of life between it and the earth life. These planes however, so intricately interpenetrate that it would take one better versed in the matter than I am to intelligently differentiate. So for convenience, we will just call it "the Power House" and let it go at that.

Evidently we were expected, as many great spirits were waiting to greet and welcome us, after which they accompanied us into the wonderful electrified building in which we had gone when there before. Again I stood on the transparent floor, again felt its pulse beating in the same way, but saw nothing as I looked down into the void toward earth, which was as a closed door. I knew that my presence was not required there and passed almost hurriedly up into the apartment where I looked upon the panorama of my earth life, where the shadow body had laid down at my feet and the light had gone out of it and disappeared into the whiteness above.

After mentally reviewing all that I had seen there I became oppressed, goaded, as it were, by the desire to go on, which became so irresistible that I looked at Meon for explanation, saying, half apologetically:

"I want to go on."

Instead of this being a discourtesy, as I half feared, it was received with great rejoicing and it was with the most elaborate ceremony that I was conducted into another part of what appeared to be the same suite, where I was greeted by the most ethereal, shadowy creatures that I had yet encountered, veritable spirits of spirits, whose soft gentleness and loving solicitude made their presence almost painful joy, while the very essence of soul music was coming from everywhere. In the center, surrounded by these beings was an opaline, couch-shaped cloud, kissed by amethyst and gold, and in obedience to my perceptions, despite its unsubstantial appearance, I reclined upon it. It was quite restfully reliable and its soft magnetic embrace very pleasing. If one can conceive of such a thing this couch gave the impression of a cloud being held together and supported by electricity but it was quite sufficient for my body, which was as ethereal as my surroundings. Reclining thereupon I wish I could adequately describe my sensations, as these wonderful creatures hovered about me, holding me in the magic of their presence, intensifying my desire to be like them. Then I was conscious of a change—an inner lightness and power, which grew into a feeling of independence of the shadow or spirit body, as though it were a part of the couch rather than myself, much as I had felt about the physical body before leaving the earth plane.

Again the great electrified current manifested itself, but this time with a quivering instead of vibrating, taking me unto itself so gently that it was almost imperceptible. Souls of the superethereal realm were calling to me, calling into a world that is as far above the ethereal as the ethereal is above the physical and I wanted to go. Then I could feel myself slipping, slipping over the borderland where the realm of God kisses the realm of Christ, to remain beyond which we must have become as Christs, as beyond it we begin the evolution toward the Ultimate —Godhood.

Then I was looking down upon my spirit body much as I had done my mundane garment after leaving it upon the earth plane, and into the grandeur of it all came a voice saying: "It is the second death," and as I wondered at the word "death," the voice explained:

"That word has no application to the soul—it applies only to its garments as they are cast aside."

There was something appealing about the little shadow body as it lay there in all its transparent whiteness amid its glistening environment—a stranger in a strange land—what would become of it? Possibly it was a gift of that plane just as the clay image is the gift of earth. Why was Meon sitting beside it —why had he not come with me? All this I was asking myself when suddenly I realized that I was a great power and began analyzing myself to see what constituted *me* and found there was no *me*— there was only *I*. Yes, I was consciously *I*, a greater Ego that I had ever been, yet I was only a little light within a misty white globe, *one* with and within the great electrified current, a veritable spirit of a spirit, a living atom of intellectual power—a power more wonderful than even my wildest dreams ever depicted. The living thing within was *memory,* an insignificant little impediment or otherwise in the earth life as we suppress it, or hold it fondly to our hearts crying out in anguish, "Oh, if I could only forget— if I could only forget." True, if we could only forget we would leave the judge, the jury and the executioner this side of the Styx! Be that as it may, memory is refined and purified and lays down its every burden before it passes into this realm, where sins, sorrows and shadows never violate. The soul is veritably stripped of every shadow, the process of which is not always a delightful diversion as we come up through the different strata of life from the earth to the "Power House," therefore, it is well for us to remember that a burden placed on memory must go on a very long journey, perhaps several of them, before the soul can free itself of it. Nothing we can do will keep the soul's tomorrow from coming but we can refrain from placing upon tomorrow burdens of today. On the other hand it is *possible,* though rarely attained, to so live the earth life that we can pass almost immediately beyond the condition through which I had just passed—the second death.

It was an exceedingly blissful condition in which I found myself, a veritable dream of Heaven; and of all the places I had ever visited in the worlds of spirit this most appealed to me. I wanted to stay and settled down with the sensation of permanency among these souls reveling in their dreams of idealty. Many were entering in and strangest of all some seemed to be going back down through the "Power House." This going back reminded me of my expressed desire in that direction and I became restless, with that "going on" feeling and almost instantly I was quivering upward within the electrified current with something of a pang at leaving the wonderful "residential section" that had so appealed to me. As we ascended so refined became the uplifting process that it was more of a perception than a movement, just floating in a void of blended harmony, enchantingly exhilarating. Feeling that I was soon to know the ultimate of a soul I began conjecturing as to its beginning. A voice, or rather a mental impression came softly out of the silence:

"Every soul is as young as the youngest; every soul is as old as the oldest; all have existed since time began." Where did the voice come from? Suddenly I realized that that which had been to me a great **electrified current was** in reality a great universal Spirit, interpenetrating everything, uniting all realms, lifting souls ever onward on the journey of evolution and progression—it was a living, intellectual, speaking entity, the great silent emissary of all power—the God spirit—a kind of universal thread on which all life is strung.

I was not the only passenger within this living, electrified elevator, whose invisible silent power was limitless, world-embracing. There were other globe-confined lights moving about blazing with luminosity, with which I recognized myself as unified yet separate, but above all was the conviction that we would yet be *one* in a greater and more concrete sense by a process yet unrevealed.

We passed through indescribable strata of space, wonderful beyond description but did not come in contact with any condition of life but went ever steadily onward, the uplifting process of which had become

> "Such a tide as, moving seems asleep
> Too full for sound and foam."

Then a living whiteness, a veritable white fire of radiance was interpenetrating everything with a neutralizing effect, giving the impression of finality —the end. There was no sense of being overpowered but just a merging into Infinitude as it merged into me—as a dewdrop sinks into the sea and the sea into the dewdrop—just a unification. I was still consciously *I* in a most remarkable sense—I felt that *I*, myself, was Infinity—a thrill inexpressible! It was the end of the journey—coming home after the endless ages of reincarnations, of battling through worlds material and ethereal, burning in the crucible of Evolution through the wearisome eons and cycles of time for the Ultimate—where evolution pours her

Gods—atoms of life unifying with the source of life.

I could see the passengers, just little lights no longer encumbered by even the misty globes, losing themselves in the Power Radiance, becoming one with it. Suddenly I remembered the earth and my request to return to it but suspended as I was between the end and the beginning of the journey, I did not dare to hope that my desire to return to earth with a story of a "far country" would be respected, as I had known so many in the spirit worlds with the same desire. Too late, we want to come back just for the good we may do but how few ever come back across the dark span!

Then I could feel the mantle of Infinitude withdrawing itself, throwing me back, as it were, into the neutralized current, rendering me as negative as I had been a moment before positive, as a soundless voice, a mentalized wave floated into my consciousness:

"Return thou unto earth chained to thy request."

In an instant a change was over everything. I was quivering within the electrified current, moving out into the Whiteness, my face toward the earth. As I looked down I seemed to see it, to feel its magnetism. In fancy, I seemed to hear it calling me, to feel that it rejoiced that I was returning and a great joy was within me that the privilege was mine and as I came on down through the quivering, silvery whiteness, still tuned with the Infinite, nothing seemed impossible. How wonderful it all was then, but now reduced to the small, material capacity of pen, ink and paper, I can only say—what havoc reality plays with our dreams!

But I was still dreaming the wonderful dream

when there came a gentle pause, a slowing vibration and suspended I was looking down upon my shadow body just where I had left it, with Meon still beside it. All about me were those superethereal beings and just for a moment I relaxed, giving myself up to the restful joy of that realm that had so appealed to me and then slipped into my spirit body so easily that I marvelled.

At first it seemed such a thing apart that it was oppressive then I could feel myself giving it life and power, renewing its life in conjunction with mine. In a little while I arose from the couch with it as much a part of me as it had ever been.

There was great rejoicing, as they all seemed to know where I had been and were pleased to regard me as a very exalted being instead of a poor mundane creature on its way back to earth. Some questioned me as to the life in the world of the Ultimate, all of which I answered as well as I might.

> "But far on the deep there are billows
>   That never shall break on the beach;
> And I have heard songs in the Silence
>   That never shall float into speech
> And I have had dreams in the Valley
>   Too lofty for language to reach."

"Meon, did you know I was coming back?" I asked eagerly.

"Yes."

"Is it well that I have done so?"

"That depends on yourself—it is a rare responsibility as well as privilege."

My soul was caressing that thrill of Infinitude and the wonderful privilege and possibilities that were mine, as we went down and stood once again on the transparent floor, felt that strange pulse beating sensation and then were going downward, floating out into space, accompanied by many great spirits, who rejoiced with us, lighting up our pathway by their self-illumination, singing in unison with the "choir invisible." My loved ones who are in the spirit world then joined us, all vibrating in joyous delirium, until a hand closed gently on mine and the voice of Meon was saying:

"Come," to which I quickly responded remembering with compassion a fast deteriorating clay image in the darkness on the far away earth and hastened downward, creeping into the cold deadness of it.

CHAPTER XXVII.

A SOUL RELINKING WITH EARTH.

So unresponsive was the stiffening clay in which I was incarcerated that I feared my long absence had forefeited my dominance over it. I labored long and earnestly with the problem of readjustment, realizing the impotency of the spirit in a material executive sense without the co-operation of the body. I was so oppressively cramped that I had to combat the desire to just let go and return into the spirit world.

> "O, Thou who hast poured the essence of thy life
> Into this urn—this feeble urn of clay."

Morning found me so indifferently adjusted that I feigned sleep until long after the breakfast hour, as I was far from being assured that I could speak, to say nothing of eating. When the nurse went out of the room and I was alone I tried my voice in a low tone, the squeaky sound of which struck me as being exceedingly comical and I laughed most heartily (noiselessly, of course). That laugh did more toward adjusting me than one could imagine. The blood began circulating with the sensation as of something crawling on me, it excelled all "flesh creeping" producers in the category of "creeping things," for the few seconds it lasted. I squirmed in the agony of it but when it was over I found that my soul and body were at least on *living* terms and I was much less oppressed. When the lunch hour came I spared myself any further comment on that subject by eating lightly, as my body had become fairly responsive and I was feeling unusually well considering everything.

As the day wore on I could not resist wandering back to the Ultimate—the fullness of Infinitude with which I still felt myself unified, the reflected glory of which seemed to make a veritable paradise of that little man-made room and all that was within it. Truly the kingdom of Heaven was within me, and I thought of the wonderful grain of truth, "I myself am Heaven and Hell," that our beloved Omar had planted in his quaint philosophy that we all love and hold tenderly to our hearts yet dare not exemplify in our lives.

When night had settled down and its shadows were flitting about mockingly I watched and waited, hoping against hope, the echo of the "good-bye," which I had heard the night before when I was leaving the spirit world haunting me with a meaning that I tried to shut out. I could not bear the thought that my pilgrimages into the spirit realms were over.

"Meon, are you there?" I called and called again into the silence but no answer came, as tears welled up ever and anon to burn the dry, deadened lids. I knew I had been given back to earth but was loath to accept it, and grew resentful because of Meon's absence, feeling that he should at least relieve my suspense by telling me the truth. His absence was really a verification of my worst apprehensions, as I knew if he did not come I would not go, as he had gone with me on every occasion of my going.

"One, two," yes, it was two o'clock and while hope was slowly dying out I became aware of touches unlike any I had ever felt on my face and hands to which I paid little attention until they extended over my entire body which until then had been practically insensible since the night of my first voyage upon the mystic sea of the silence. To have sensibility return after so long a time should have pleased but instead I could have cried aloud in the anguish of its recognized meaning. I had known the life of a spirit —had ridden on the wings of evolution to its finality and now to take up the burden of physical existence again seemed an impossible thing despite the fact that I had so ardently desired it. The dream and the reality!

This touching, as of fingers, continued, pressing upon me, growing ever more vigorous. I thought of the earth-magnetized spirits I had seen groping about in the spirit darkness and shuddered but my perception assured me that I had nothing to fear from these as they were not of the submerged type but beneficial in some indefinable way. But what were they doing—what did they mean?

At last I perceived Meon and cried out to him:

"Meon, what is this that keeps picking on me?"

"You are in the hands of the healers and will soon be well."

"Healers?" I echoed in astonishment, wondering that such seemingly material methods should be resorted to, and asked, "Why could that not be done spiritually?"

"Your body has fallen out of accommodation or co-operation with your spirit and practically become a material substance, therefore, is being treated as such in remagnetizing it."

"Why could not *I* remagnetize it with spiritual co-operation?"

"You could if you *wanted* to but you do not and

there is no time to be lost where it is concerned. These manipulations will persist until you turn your mind to the restoration of your body, which is, for the present, your home. The object of your indisposition is over and there is nothing to hinder your speedy recovery."

"Am I never to come out again?" I wailed despairingly.

As I waited listening eagerly I seemed to hear that sentence that had so haunted me—"Weaver of thy freedom, be faithful," following in its wake came another, "Return thou unto earth chained to thy request," and veritable I felt chained—hopelessly chained but after a few minutes of "kicking against the pricks," I reasoned with and coaxed myself into a resignation that I did not altogether feel. I reasoned that I had been given what I most ardently desired and should be rejoicing instead of complaining, wondering at my own inconsistency. Thus began the relinking of a soul with a body from which it had been released in the pursuit of the brand of knowledge that St. Mark doubtless meant when he said, "There is nothing hid that shall not be manifested."

As the days went on the "healers" worked with admirable persistence and I could feel myself growing stronger and stronger, until I could recognize my body as a part of myself just as it had been before the separation came, "even as you and I"—just as any of us feel, for which I was sometimes glad—sometimes sorrowful, for it was not easy to tear oneself away from the lure of the "other side," so beautifully different. Yet the spirit world has its obligations and lessons just as the earth life and we can never get so far nor become so highly evolved that we do not recognize the earth life as the greatest opportunity of the soul and should use it accordingly instead of abusing it, as we too often do.

Earth naturally exacts its obligations, its toll, just as any plane does. At the same time we must consider its beautiful gifts, privileges and opportunities —all ours for the taking. It gives of itself a body in which to clothe our spirit, which body it maintains by the products of its industry. By the strong arm of its gravitation it holds us in safety to itself. We use its gifts of clay to do our bidding and according to such servitude our spirits progress and grow in strength, usefulness and helpfulness, and, finally, when it has served our purposes we give it back without even a feeling of thankfulness or realization of the wonderful opportunities it has afforded our spirits. Even where the spirit becomes the servant and the clay the master, earth is not to blame but rather the weakness of the spirit to be pitied. When earth life is lived in accordance with the laws and privileges governing it, other phases of life follow automatically and with as little friction as day follows night.

To strengthen us, to force us into the mastery, earth permits us to burn in the caldrons of her temptations, to fall over her precipices, always recognizing:

"Great souls must burn in sorrow's furnace heat
    Ere fully fitted life's great work to meet."

Earth life is one of the strongest links in the great co-operative chain of evolution, and in the light of geological teachings and surmises, et cetera, who can say that our dear old mother earth is not, herself, some great soul ploughing the heavy sea of evolution toward—what?

So rapid was my improvement that within a few days I went, accompanied by my fiance and the nurse, for a drive on the beach. How vividly I recall every incident—someway it stands out alone—different from all other outings. I was lifted down the stairs and into the yard where the sunshine touched me for the first time in many long weeks—its heat was consuming. I went slowly, leaning heavily, my limbs so long unaccustomed to duty threatening to collapse at every step. When I sat down in the car it was like falling through space and ending in a crumpled heap, so completely did relaxation follow the exertion.

How strange everything seemed as we went speeding out over the city! Houses, conveyances and people seemed so unreal that I realized I had been living in the spirit so long that the physical had become the *unreal* and the spirit the *real*. I could see the spirits more plainly than I could the human beings. As my acquaintances expressed their pleasure at my convalescence and chatted of the commonplaces their voices grated on me, so unreal and harsh compared with the soft vibrating voices of the space world, which are as soft as the silence and as caressing as love.

Gradually this sense of unreality passed away. When we reached the Boulevard on the seawall level, high above the sea, I looked out over the broad expanse, where the gold of the setting sun kissed the blue of the sea. My old love for the sea welled up anew in my heart as I thought that all the beauty was not reserved for the worlds beyond ours. Watching the smoke of an outgoing steamer, far out beyond the bar, and another ploughing heavily, coming in, I was struck with the realization that on earth, just as on other planes, life is very much a matter of coming and going—not so different after all.

This drive having no ontoward results paved the way for a duplication every afternoon and a very long one on Sunday—to the very end of the island. After our return I could not disguise from myself that I was very tired, which being patent to every one was accepted as a natural consequence of the unusual exertion.

There was one sentence that struck me forcibly, yet without any special meaning or conviction but I have recalled it often since. Just as we drove upon the sea wall facing the sun a voice cried out:

"Look into the face of the Sun and you look into the face of God."

It was not, however, until I was alone that I realized how very tired I was and lay down without removing my clothes. Instead of resting there came upon me the perversity of unrest, rendering relaxation impossible as I tossed and sighed in the distress of it. Then Meon stood beside me and I implored him:

"Oh, Meon, I am so tired I cannot rest here—do let me come out and float about in cool comfortable space and I will feel so different—please."

"Rest where you are," came with gentle firmness, as a sense of finality pressed upon me—the full realization that I had been given back to earth unreservedly, to which I would have protested perhaps but there was a pain, the very essence of pain, as of something being withdrawn from my right side just below the ribs in the identical spot where I had felt the thrust or impact the first night my soul was released and I went over the borderland. This excruciating pain—and it was the most acute I ever remember in all my life—spread over my entire body interpenetrating it, enveloping it, with an agony beyond endurance, then gradually subsided, leaving only a soreness centralized in a small area in the side. After it subsided and I relaxed from the agony of it, there was upon me the sense of my soul and body having been locked together again—made one—an atom of infinitude and an image of clay. Following this almost immediately was severe internal bleeding, the blood of which was dark, clotted and stagnant in appearance, which forced me to remain for days with ice bottles on the affected side, keeping it in a frozen condition. Here is where the doctor and the nurse exercised their prerogative relentlessly, enforcing an invalidism that tried my patience to the utmost. Nor did the "healers" grow weary of "well doing"—they persisted until I was in such a condition of physical supersensitiveness that anything touching my skin distressed it—especially those ice bottles. During these trying days the invisible forces did not desert me but instead hovered about with loving solicitude telling beautiful stories (and otherwise) of other worlds and their experiences therein.

Of all the *unreal* things in this tangled web of unreality, this connecting link, in a *physical* way, between the release of my soul from the body and its final return, days later, is the most unreal—the most inexplicable. I even hesitate to embody it but as it is as much a link in this chain of mystery as any of the other incidents, I feel inclined to so respect it.

Then came a day, a beautiful summer's day, when I pulled myself away from the shadows of other worlds and took my place in the world of human affairs where I had left off more than two months before, a consciously reincarnated being—the same and yet how different!

CHAPTER XXVIII.

AS THE TODAYS BECAME YESTERDAYS.

As people congratulated me on my return from the "valley of the shadow," I wondered what they would think if they knew just how far beyond the "valley" I had penetrated, and at times smiled bitterly as I realized with what incredulity such a statement would be received.

This, however, did not alter my resolve to write and I began to wonder just how much had already been written on the subject and what information was available. This I determined to ascertain and avail myself of the reading thereof, feeling that if some one else had written frankly on such a subject it might lessen the full burden of criticism that I felt would descend on me for daring to stray so far from the "calf paths" made by the few minds who "belled" themselves for the herd to follow. Meon silenced all further conjecture by interrupting emphatically:

"Read no line on this subject until you have written—then you will be free to read as you will."

"Why?" I asked in surprise, wondering what difference it could make, feeling assured that it could in no way affect me.

"Writings are always clothed in the personality of the writer and errors of personality often unconsciously intrude themselves upon truth. The truths that have been given to you will tax your personality to the very utmost without seeking the errors of others that are already clad."

While I resented this, in a way, I have abided by

it conscientiously and refrained from taking up any phase of the subject. Otherwise, possibly I would never have written as I have—taking, as it were, a naked truth and clothing it in words that fit in some places and misfit glaringly in others. However, the clothing of the ethereal in material form is rather a delicate process, the superlativeness of which only experience can demonstrate, as the ethereal must come down to the material—the material cannot be lifted up to it.

As I grew stronger the invisible forces did not withdraw their interest but watched over me even more eagerly, permitting me to feel the pleasure of their solicitude, which did much to promote the restoration of my health and by the end of August I was practically well, despite a peculiar all-over weakness which spirit communication imposed upon me at times.

Then my fiance became my husband, and the great wedding that was to have been, was conspicuous by its simplicity. A traveling dress of champagne-colored messaline made rather a pretty substitute for the magnificent pearl-bedecked creation that had so injected itself into that weird drama of the shadows.

I was physically unequal to the Oriental tour we had planned and after remaining in New Orleans a few days stress of business called my husband back to Galveston, where we remained only a short time before launching our ship of business in other waters, where the tides of more than two years have ebbed and flowed with my resolution to write riding on the uncertain wave of "someday," with the sunshine of love blinding me to the universal law of duty.

"Yes, I will write it all some day," I would assure my accusing conscience (that "still small voice" within), while I "gloried and drank deep" at the Court of Procrastination, wearing the crown of Love, studded with jewels of contentment, while the days with their wonderful opportunities passed unheeded into the file of yesterdays.

As I grew stronger I half feared my ability to communicate with the world invisible would abate accordingly but that rare privilege is still mine and my health was never so splendid in all my life. However, it is a prerogative I rarely exercise but that it is mine to use when I elect lends a significance to life that nothing can take away and nothing else can give. Be that as it may, on the whole that experience is one I would not care to duplicate, nor obliterate, as during those days I lived consciously and intelligently in two worlds, as much in one as in the other, in neither and yet in both, drinking to the dregs the cup of agony as well as joy.

It was at night when all the world was sleeping and "silence, that dreadful bell" was ringing sombrely that Meon and the great spirits would come and chide me with their mute reproaches. Respecting the law of self-responsibility they would not speak but my soul would cry out self-condemned in the agony of the unredeemed promise that I had laid upon it while in the world of shadows and I would renew my assurances, but when daylight came everything seemed so different that I just drifted with the difference—assuring myself that the world was not ready for such knowledge. And then there was my husband's attitude on the subject!

Finally the ghost of that unexecuted promise to which my soul seemed veritably chained, began haunting me both day and night, taking all the joy out of life, filling me with an unrest that nothing could dissipate, and my mind was ever reverting responsively to Schiller's abjuration: "Why hast thou cast me thus into the town of the ever-blind to proclaim thine oracle with the opened sense? Take back this clear-sightedness; take from mine eyes this cruel light! Give me back my blindness—the happy darkness of my senses; take back thy dreadful gift!"

Then came a spring night, cool with a touch of winter in it, the wind howled dismally and I tossed in the anguish of "murdered sleep." I could see the light burning in my husband's room and knew that he, too, was restless and reading, as is his custom when he cannot sleep. We had come in late from a box party at the theatre and I was miserably tired and sleepy but this did not matter to the invisibles who waited to administer their mute reproaches, which seemed more unbearable than ever before. I tried to shut them out with the same old promises, which they heeded not but just waited—waited in the stillness of the night as I lay in the torture of sleepless self-condemnation.

Then from afar came soft strains of the "choir invisible," and upon me was the awareness of little electric shocks. How well I remember them! Yes, there was the great electrified current coming down upon me, touching me, gathering me unto itself, just as it had done before. The horror seized me that it was death that had come, that I had forfeited the opportunity so ardently sought and my soul was crying out with the renewal of the promise it meant to redeem regardless of all things—everything.

No spirit word was spoken—no sound broke the awesome stillness—I could feel myself clasped within the vibrations of the great electrified current moving upward, going up bodily just as I had once before; I could feel the covers slipping away as they fell back on the bed, hear the bells of my little dog's collar jingle as he hurried about excitedly, a benumbing cold permeating everything. I was vibrating slowly upward, up, up. One hand was resting on my breast, the other hanging limply down, eyes closed, and a hopeless resignation pressing heavily upon me. Then came a pause and I apprehensively opened my eyes to behold a wondrous change. I was staring into a white-canvas-like mist fringed by a nebulosity in which variegated colors played, the blue of electricity predominating. As in a moving picture I saw myself on the train with Meon beside me, just as on that May morning which seemed so long ago. Following this was a panorama of every incident in the weird, shadowy drama in which Fate had sent me far wandering into the realm whose door is death. As I viewed it thus condensed, I realized more forcibly than ever the intricately intimate relationship of the realms, visible and invisible, each a continuation of the other, each interpenetrating and all interpenetrated by that great electrified current, making "one stupendous whole." When the wonderful moving scene, which so enthralled me, came to the relinking of the soul with earth I could feel myself being lowered, vibrating downward, my eyes fastened on the slowly fading scene until the clouds broke into rolling confusion and there came into the shadowy mist, in letters of gold, these words:

"'Twas not given for you alone
Pass it on; Pass it on."

THE END.

Since writing the foregoing I have come to the conclusion that Agassiz was not very far wrong when he said:

"Every great scientific truth goes through three stages. First people say it conflicts with the Bible. Next they say it has been discovered before. Lastly they say they have always believed it."

For the convenience of those who may be thus influenced I submit the following Bible references covering different phases of spirit manifestation:

INDEPENDENT SPIRIT VOICES.

Matthew, iii, 16, 17	Matthew, xvii, 5	John, xii, 28, 29, 30
Ezekiel, i, 28	Mark, ix, 7	I Sam., iii, 3, 9
Acts, xi, 7, 8, 9	Deut., ix, 12, 13	Acts, ix, 4-7
Job, iv, 1-6		

SPIRIT LEVITATION.

II Kings, ii, 9, 10, 11	I Kings, xviii, 12	Ezekiel, viii, 3
Acts, viii, 39	Ezekiel, iii, 12, 13, 14	

SPIRIT COMMUNICATIONS IN DREAMS.

Job, xxxiii, 15	Joel, ii, 28	Genesis, xxxi, 11
Genesis, xxxvii, 5	Genesis, xxviii, 12	

SPIRIT CONTROL OR INFLUENCE.

Numbers, xxiv, 4	Acts, ix, 3, 9	Daniel, viii, 18
Daniel, x, 9	Genesis, xv, 12, 17	I Kings, xiv, 5
Acts, x, 10, 11	Acts, xxii, 17	

MATERIALIZATION.

Matthew, xvii, 1, 9	Job, iv, 15	Ezekiel, ii, 9
Genesis, xviii, 1	Exodus, xxiv, 10, 11	Mark, ix, 4
Luke, xxiv, 15, 16, 29, 30, 31	John, xx, 19, 20	Genesis, iii, 8
	Genesis, xxxii, 24	Daniel, v, 5

WRITING.

II Chron., xxi, 12	Exodus, xxxiv, 1	Exodus, xxxi, 18
Exodus, xxxii, 16	Exodus, xxiv, 12	Duet., ix, 10
Daniel, v, 5	Duet., v, 22	

TESTS.

Matt., xxvii, 51, 52, 53	Judges, vi, 36, 40	I Sam., i, 10, 11, 17,
Genesis, xxiv, 14, 19	I Sam., x, 2, 10	26, 27, 28
Job, iv, 15, 16, 17		

"For He is not a God of the dead but of the living; for all live unto Him."—Luke, xx, 38.

"Concerning spiritual gifts brethren I would not have you ignorant."—I Cor., xii, 1.

Also I find many who are influenced by what *others* think, and grade the subject accordingly. Such persons may be as much surprised as I was to find that a very long list of our foremost writers, teachers, thinkers, scientists and philosophers (past and present) are not only liberal where spirit phenomena is concerned but have written openly admitting that there is something in it, notable among whom are two of the world's greatest scientists, Sir Oliver Lodge and Sir William Crookes.